Framing Civic Engagement, Political Participation and Active Citizenship in Europe

Edited by
Cristiano Bee and Roberta Guerrina

LONDON AND NEW YORK

First published 2015 by Routledge

2 Park Square, Milton Park, Abingdon, Oxfordshire OX14 4RN
711 Third Avenue, New York, NY 10017

Routledge is an imprint of the Taylor & Francis Group, an informa business

First issued in paperback 2018

Copyright © 2015 Taylor & Francis

All rights reserved. No part of this book may be reprinted or reproduced or utilised in any form or by any electronic, mechanical, or other means, now known or hereafter invented, including photocopying and recording, or in any information storage or retrieval system, without permission in writing from the publishers.

Notice:
Product or corporate names may be trademarks or registered trademarks, and are used only for identification and explanation without intent to infringe.

British Library Cataloguing in Publication Data
A catalogue record for this book is available from the British Library

ISBN 13: 978-1-138-82860-5 (hbk)
ISBN 13: 978-1-138-37955-8 (pbk)

Typeset in Times New Roman
by RefineCatch Limited, Bungay, Suffolk

Publisher's Note
The publisher accepts responsibility for any inconsistencies that may have arisen during the conversion of this book from journal articles to book chapters, namely the possible inclusion of journal terminology.

Disclaimer
Every effort has been made to contact copyright holders for their permission to reprint material in this book. The publishers would be grateful to hear from any copyright holder who is not here acknowledged and will undertake to rectify any errors or omissions in future editions of this book.

Contents

Citation Information   vii

1. Introduction: Framing Civic Engagement, Political Participation and Active Citizenship in Europe   1
   Cristiano Bee & Roberta Guerrina

2. Political and Civic Engagement and Participation: Towards an Integrative Perspective   5
   Martyn Barrett & Ian Brunton-Smith

3. Participation, Dialogue, and Civic Engagement: Understanding the Role of Organized Civil Society in Promoting Active Citizenship in the European Union   29
   Cristiano Bee & Roberta Guerrina

4. Europe as a Beacon of Democracy? Citizenship Policies Relating to Youth and Migrants in Portugal   51
   Norberto Ribeiro, Carla Malafaia, Maria Fernandes-Jesus, Tiago Neves & Isabel Menezes

5. Civic and Political Participation of Women and Youth in Turkey: An Examination of Perspectives of Public Authorities and NGOs   69
   Tulin Sener

6. On Active Citizenship: Discourses and Language about Youth and Migrants in Italy   82
   Paola Villano & Alberto Bertocchi

7. Active Citizenship in the UK: Assessing Institutional Political Strategies and Mechanisms of Civic Engagement   100
   Cristiano Bee & Dimitra Pachi

Index   119

Citation Information

The chapters in this book were originally published in the *Journal of Civil Society*, volume 10, issue 1 (April 2014). When citing this material, please use the original page numbering for each article, as follows:

Chapter 1
Introduction: Framing Civic Engagement, Political Participation and Active Citizenship in Europe
Cristiano Bee & Roberta Guerrina
Journal of Civil Society, volume 10, issue 1 (April 2014) pp. 1–4

Chapter 2
Political and Civic Engagement and Participation: Towards an Integrative Perspective
Martyn Barrett & Ian Brunton-Smith
Journal of Civil Society, volume 10, issue 1 (April 2014) pp. 5–28

Chapter 3
Participation, Dialogue, and Civic Engagement: Understanding the Role of Organized Civil Society in Promoting Active Citizenship in the European Union
Cristiano Bee & Roberta Guerrina
Journal of Civil Society, volume 10, issue 1 (April 2014) pp. 29–50

Chapter 4
Europe as a Beacon of Democracy? Citizenship Policies Relating to Youth and Migrants in Portugal
Norberto Ribeiro, Carla Malafaia, Maria Fernandes-Jesus, Tiago Neves & Isabel Menezes
Journal of Civil Society, volume 10, issue 1 (April 2014) pp. 51–68

Chapter 5
Civic and Political Participation of Women and Youth in Turkey: An Examination of Perspectives of Public Authorities and NGOs
Tulin Sener
Journal of Civil Society, volume 10, issue 1 (April 2014) pp. 69–81

CITATION INFORMATION

Chapter 6
On Active Citizenship: Discourses and Language about Youth and Migrants in Italy
Paola Villano & Alberto Bertocchi
Journal of Civil Society, volume 10, issue 1 (April 2014) pp. 82–99

Chapter 7
Active Citizenship in the UK: Assessing Institutional Political Strategies and Mechanisms of Civic Engagement
Cristiano Bee & Dimitra Pachi
Journal of Civil Society, volume 10, issue 1 (April 2014) pp. 100–117

Please direct any queries you may have about the citations to clsuk.permissions@cengage.com

INTRODUCTION

Framing Civic Engagement, Political Participation and Active Citizenship in Europe

CRISTIANO BEE & ROBERTA GUERRINA

School of Politics, University of Surrey, Guildford, UK

This special issue evaluates the role that civic engagement, political participation, and active citizenship can play in promoting the establishment of a European polity. The articles included here examine how the practice of active citizenship is managed and constructed in the context of a European drive to increase civic engagement and political participation in three member states (Portugal, Italy, and the UK) and one accession country (Turkey). Looking at both processes and policies promoting active citizenship at the European and national levels, this special issue uncovers current discourses as well as political priorities and values that surround the activities of nongovernmental organizations (NGOs). Of particular interest are debates about the nature and level of civic and political participation and engagement of marginal groups (women, youths, migrants, and minorities) as they are particularly vulnerable to social exclusion.

The literature on civic and political participation and engagement focuses on the failure of traditional policy approaches to engender higher levels of ownership and participation within the European polity. This trend is more acute in relation to marginal groups. Both Fraser (1992) and Laclau and Mouffe (1985) have called for a re-valuation of the relationship between public and private spheres in order to understand the mechanisms and nature of civic and political participation and the role that discourse plays in establishing dominant notions of political concepts. From this perspective, traditional conceptualizations of the public sphere have served to frame our understandings of ownership and participation. This theoretical framework informs the way our special issue looks at the role of political discourse in shaping policy outcomes and associated responses. The articles included here compare institutional and civil society approaches to active citizenship in order to make sense of convergence, fragmentation, and hierarchies of power in the construction of political identities amongst traditionally marginal groups.

The wider political context within which 'policies on active citizenship' have entered the public domain frames the scope and aims of the activities and programmes falling under this broad umbrella. This analysis draws on a long-standing debate about the role and position of citizens in shaping the European integration process. Historically, the EU has struggled to consolidate a coherent citizenship programme (Follesdal, 2001; Kostakopoulou, 2008). Despite calls for a more coherent approach to post-national citizenship through various public information, and education and cultural campaigns, the results have been disappointing (Nicolaïdis, 2013; Shore, 2012). Recent events relating to austerity highlight the continued relevance of this research agenda that is more and more concentrated on debates about the democratic deficit and decision-making processes at the European level.

From an institutional perspective, building a more legitimate European project has to be based on open and dialogic participation and communication practices (CEC, 2005, 2006). This strategy is evident in the inclusion of Article 11 in the Lisbon Treaty. The establishment of a wider basis for the participation and engagement of stakeholders' networks, NGOs, and other non-state actors that form the backbone of European civil society is at the very core of this initiative. Active citizenship, the representation of local policy actors at the supranational level, and strategies for civic engagement and empowerment of civil society become benchmarks for evaluating the impact of Europeanization at the national and local levels. The values associated with active citizenship and the significance attributed to it are recognized in the political discourse promoted by public institutions in the different countries that we compare in our special issue, showing that the need to promote civic engagement and political participation is acknowledged as a policy response to a number of social problems (such as discrimination, racism, social exclusion, lack of integration between communities, etc.).

The 'empowerment of civil society' has thus become a key political priority not only for the European Commission but also for many public institutions across Europe. The core argument of this special issue is that this process is favoured by two interrelated dimensions: (1) the increase in civil society organizations' cooperation and engagement in transnational networks and (2) the shaping of a civil dialogue between NGOs and public institutions across Europe.

The special issue focuses on the interaction between institutions and civil society actors, addressing a number of questions related to their reciprocal role in influencing, shaping, criticizing, or disregarding certain political priorities. More specifically the articles in the special issue provide, on a comparative basis, insights regarding three interrelated levels of analysis.

First of all, the special issue provides an overview of current understandings of civic and political participation. In their article, Barrett and Brunton-Smith rely on a secondary analysis of existing data sets (such as European Social Survey and Eurobarometer) in order to unpack the complexity inherent to the different factors that enable or hinder political and civic participation. Their contribution calls for the reframing of current theoretical approaches and for the enhancement of the focus on both psychological characteristics and social circumstances that is necessary for the definition of new integrative approaches to study active citizenship.

Second, the special issue looks at the development of active citizenship at the EU level. The analysis provided by Bee and Guerrina reviews the complexity of the different dynamics of power that characterize the shaping of specific discourses regarding civic engagement and political participation by the European Commission and by NGOs in Brussels. More specifically, the article looks at the counter-discourses produced by organizations representing traditionally marginalized groups in respect to official discourses that represent European institutions' political needs.

Finally, the special issue concentrates on the emergence of specific public discourses surrounding active citizenship in four European countries (Portugal, Turkey, Italy, and the UK) and explores the meaning of active citizenship for activists of organizations targeting marginal groups. The article by Ribeiro et al. provides a detailed account of institutional dynamics that surround the shaping of a political discourse regarding active citizenship in Portugal. The article looks at the institutional priorities that have emerged in the country and at their overall alignment with European policies and values. The authors unpack some of the contradictions that surround civic engagement and political participation: on one side, activists fully recognize the institutional attempts to shape policies that activate the engagement of marginalized groups, whilst, on the other side, they point to the lack of actual impact of these policies. The article by Sener provides an overview of official public institutions' and civil society discourses in Turkey by looking predominantly at women and young people. The analysis provides evidence of the high level of associationalism that characterizes the country, represented by a multi-layered set of voluntary organizations. This, however, does not correspond to an actual empowerment of the organizations representing these social groups in respect to the institutional level. Villano and Bertocchi provide an outline of the institutional and civil society discourses on active citizenship in official legislation in Italy and outline the perceptions of mechanisms for civic engagement and political participation of activists of organizations representing youth and minorities. Their analysis outlines a number of key issues that are central for establishing and improving active citizenship in a country that has traditionally been characterized by high levels of associationalism but has recently experienced a decline in civic and political participation. Bee and Pachi focus on the emergence of the debate regarding active citizenship in the UK. The analysis provides a comparison between different ideological definitions of active citizenship, as they emerged in the New Right and New Labour political discourses. The investigation focuses on activists representing various NGOs involved in activities with different social groups and on their political values, political orientations, and criticism of current institutional approaches to active citizenship.

The special issue provides an overview of practices and responses to recent institutional demands to increase civic engagement, political participation, and active citizenship across Europe. In this regard, our research takes account of bottom-up processes of active citizenship and puts particular emphasis on the activists' point of view, their political values and priorities, and their actual practice of engagement. The articles draw on the work of a project looking at Processes Influencing Democratic Ownership and Participation (PIDOP) in Europe, sponsored by the European Commission's 7th Framework Programme (FP7-SSH-2007-1, Grant Agreement no. 225282). They have hugely benefitted from the constant interaction with a number of practitioners as well as peer academics that have participated in the outreach activities that we planned throughout the project. In this regard, we would like to thank Giovanni Moro (FONDACA-Active Citizenship Foundation, Italy), Udo C. Enwereuzor (COSPE, Italy), Jan Husak (Czech Council of Children and Youth, Czech Republic), Annette Lawson (National Alliance of Women's

Organisations, UK), and Reinhild Otte (Council of Europe, France) for their participation at the *Roundtable on Active Citizenship in Europe* that took place at the University of Bologna in May 2011. We would also like to thank Bryony Hoskins (University of Southampton, UK) and Monica Threlfall (London Metropolitan University, UK) for their contributions in the panel on *Active Citizenship and Political Participation* that we organized at the final PIDOP conference that took place at the University of Surrey in April 2012. Finally, we would like to thank the anonymous reviewers who provided constructive comments on these articles.

References

CEC (2005) *The Commission's Contribution to the Period of Reflection and Beyond: Plan-D for Democracy, Dialogue and Debate*, COM (2005) 494 final. Brussels: Commission of the European Communities.

CEC (2006) *White Paper on a European Communication Policy*, COM (2006) 35 final. Brussels: Commission of the European Communities.

Follesdal, A. (2001) Union citizenship; unpacking the beast of burden, *Arena Working Papers WP 01/9*, Arena Centre for European Studies, University of Oslo.

Fraser, N. (1992) Rethinking the public sphere: a contribution to the critique of actually existing democracy, in: C. Calhoun (Ed.) *Habermas and the Public Sphere*, pp. 109–142 (Cambridge, MA: MIT Press).

Kostakopoulou, D. (2008) The evolution of European Union citizenship, *European Political Science*, 7(3), pp. 285–295.

Laclau, E. & Mouffe, C. (1985) *Hegemony and Socialist Strategy: Towards a Radical Democratic Politics* (London: Verso).

Nicolaïdis, K. (2013) European demoicracy and its crisis, *Journal of Common Market Studies Volume*, 51(2), pp. 351–369.

Shore, C. (2012) The euro crisis and European citizenship: The euro 2001–2012 – celebration or commemoration? *Anthropology Today*, 28(2), pp. 5–9.

Political and Civic Engagement and Participation: Towards an Integrative Perspective

MARTYN BARRETT* & IAN BRUNTON-SMITH**

*School of Psychology, University of Surrey, Surrey, UK; **Department of Sociology, University of Surrey, Surrey, UK

ABSTRACT   *This article presents an overview of current understandings in the study of political and civic engagement and participation, drawing in particular on innovations which have emerged from the Processes Influencing Democratic Ownership and Participation (PIDOP) project. For the purposes of the article, 'engagement' is defined as having an interest in, paying attention to, or having knowledge, beliefs, opinions, attitudes, or feelings about either political or civic matters, whereas 'participation' is defined in terms of political and civic participatory behaviours. The different forms that political and civic engagement and participation can take are outlined, and the factors that are related to different patterns of engagement and participation are reviewed. These factors operate at different levels, and include distal macro contextual factors, demographic factors, proximal social factors, and endogenous psychological factors. An integrative model covering all four levels of factors is outlined. Some findings from the secondary analysis of existing data-sets (including the European Social Survey and the International Social Survey Programme) in the PIDOP project are also reported. These findings show that engagement and participation vary as a function of complex interactions between macro, demographic, and psychological factors. It is argued that multi-level integrative theories, such as the one proposed in the current article, are required to understand the drivers of political and civic engagement and participation, and that policies and interventions aimed at enhancing citizens' levels of engagement and participation need to take this multi-level complexity into account.*

This article reports some of the theoretical understandings and empirical findings which have emerged from the Processes Influencing Democratic Ownership and Participation (PIDOP) project. This research project, which was funded by the European Commission under the Seventh Framework Programme, investigated political and civic engagement and participation in nine European countries.[1]

A conceptual distinction was drawn in the project between political and civic participation. The term 'political participation' was used to refer to activity that has the intent or effect of influencing either regional, national, or supranational governance, either directly by affecting the making or implementation of public policy or indirectly by influencing the selection of individuals who make that policy (definition adapted from Verba et al., 1995). By contrast, the term 'civic participation' was used to refer to voluntary activity focused on helping others, achieving a public good or solving a community problem, including work undertaken either alone or in cooperation with others in order to effect change (definition adapted from Zukin et al., 2006).

A further conceptual distinction was drawn between 'participation' and 'engagement'. 'Participation' was construed as being behavioural in nature and so the term was used to refer to participatory behaviours. By contrast, 'engagement' was construed in psychological rather than behavioural terms and was used to denote having an interest in, paying attention to, or having knowledge, beliefs, opinions, attitudes, or feelings about either political or civic matters.

This article falls into two main sections. The first section outlines the various forms that political and civic engagement and participation can take, and provides a review of the numerous macro, demographic, social, and psychological factors that can drive political and civic engagement and participation. This first section is based upon findings that have been reported in the existing research literature. The second section of the article provides a summary of some findings which have emerged from the secondary analysis of existing data-sets in the PIDOP project. The second section thus reports original findings from the project.

A Review of Existing Findings in the Research Literature

The Different Forms of Political and Civic Engagement and Participation

Political participation takes a number of different forms, including both conventional forms which involve electoral processes (e.g. voting, election campaigning, etc.) and non-conventional forms which occur outside electoral processes (e.g. signing petitions, participating in political demonstrations, etc.). Civic participation also entails diverse types of activities, including working collectively to solve community problems, belonging to community organizations, attending meetings about issues of concern, volunteering, making donations to charities, etc. Likewise, engagement involves a range of different forms, including paying attention to the news media (newspapers, magazines, television, radio, Internet), having political or civic knowledge or beliefs, understanding political or civic values, and holding opinions about and attitudes towards political or civic matters.

Table 1 lists the numerous forms that political and civic participation and engagement may take. It should be noted that participation and engagement may be exhibited in relationship to a number of different community and institutional levels, including the local, municipal, regional, national, transnational, and supranational level. It is important to acknowledge this wide range of forms and levels if the goal is to obtain an accurate understanding of people's actual patterns of engagement and participation. This is because the exclusion of particular forms will lead to underestimations, especially

Table 1. Some of the different forms of conventional political participation, non-conventional political participation, civic participation, and political and civic engagement

Forms of conventional political participation
- Voting
- Membership of a political party
- Running for political election
- Working on political election campaigns for candidates or parties
- Donations to political parties
- Trying to persuade others to vote

Forms of non-conventional political participation
- Protests, demonstrations, marches
- Signing petitions
- Writing letters/emails to politicians or public officials
- Writing letters/emails/phone calls with a political content to the media (both old and new media)
- Writing articles/blogs with a political content for the media (both old and new media)
- Using social networking sites on the Internet to join or like groups which have a political focus
- Using social networking sites on the Internet to distribute or share links which have a political content to friends and contacts
- Wearing or displaying a symbol or sign representing support for a political cause
- Distributing leaflets which express support for a political cause
- Participating in fundraising events for a political cause
- Writing graffiti on walls which expresses support for a political cause
- Participating in other illegal actions (e.g. burning a national flag, throwing stones, rioting, etc.) in support of a political cause
- Membership of political lobbying and campaigning organizations/attending meetings of these organizations/expressing one's point of view at these meetings/participating in the activities of these organizations/holding an office in these organizations

Forms of civic participation
- Informally assisting the well-being of others in the community
- Community problem solving through community organizations/membership of community organizations/attending meetings of these organizations/expressing one's point of view at these meetings/participating in the activities of these organizations/holding an office in these organizations
- Membership of other non-political organizations (e.g. religious institutions, sports clubs, etc.)/ attending meetings of these organizations/expressing one's point of view at these meetings/ participating in the activities of these organizations/holding an office in these organizations
- School-based community service
- Undertaking organized voluntary work
- Translation and form-filling assistance for non-native speakers
- Sending remittances to others living elsewhere
- Donations to charities
- Fundraising activities for good causes
- Consumer activism: Boycotting and preferential buying

Forms of political and civic engagement
- Paying attention to the news media (newspapers, magazines, television, radio, Internet)
- Following political or civic affairs
- Having political or civic knowledge or beliefs
- Having political or civic skills
- Understanding political or civic institutions
- Understanding political or civic values
- Holding opinions about, and attitudes towards, political or civic matters
- Having feelings about political or civic matters

among particular subgroups. For example, excluding translation activities and transnational remittances is likely to lead to the underestimation of levels of participation among minority and migrant groups (Stepick *et al.*, 2008; Vertovec, 2009).

Factors Related to Patterns of Engagement and Participation

There has now been a considerable body of research into the factors that are related to different forms of engagement and participation. This research has revealed that engagement and participation are linked to distal macro contextual factors, demographic factors, proximal social factors, and endogenous psychological factors. Here, we provide a brief review of some of the principal factors which have been identified to date.

Macro contextual factors. Macro contextual factors that have been found to be related to patterns of engagement and participation include: The design of the electoral system; the population characteristics of a country; the structure and design of the political institutions within a country; and the historical, economic, and cultural characteristics of a country.

For example, various features of the *electoral system* are related to the likelihood that people will vote in an election. Voter turnout varies according to whether the electoral system uses proportional representation or a first-past-the-post system (Geys, 2006; Jackman, 1987; Jackman & Miller, 1995), whether voting is compulsory or optional (Geys, 2006; Jackman, 1987; Mattila, 2003; Smith, 1999), whether voter registration processes are simple or cumbersome (Caldeira *et al.*, 1985; Highton & Wolfinger, 1998; Powell, 1986), whether voting takes place on a rest day or on a working day (Mattila, 2003), and whether multiple elections are held concurrently on the same day or not (Geys, 2006; Smith, 1999). Voter turnout is higher when the electoral system employs proportional representation, compulsory voting, simple registration procedures, voting on a rest day, and concurrent ballots.

Three *population features* have also been found to be related to voter turnout in elections (Geys, 2006): The size of the population (the larger the electorate, the lower the electoral turnout); population stability (the more stable the population, the higher the level of voting); and the size of the minority share of the total population (the higher the minority share, the lower the voter turnout). This last finding is not a result of minority individuals being less likely to vote than majority individuals, because it has also been found that minority individuals are as likely to vote in elections as majority individuals once demographic differences are controlled (Bobo & Gilliam, 1990). Instead, the explanation seems to be that as the proportion of minority individuals in a population increases, minority voting also increases while majority voting decreases, thereby reducing voter turnout overall (Oberholzer-Gee & Waldfogel, 2001).

There is also evidence that *the structure and design of political institutions* within a country are linked to patterns of participation. For example, the specific forms of participation which are used by citizens have been found to be related to political–institutional design. Thus, citizens living in decentralized polities in which the state is relatively weak in the sense that power is not concentrated in one centre and there are a large number of access points for non-state actors to exert an influence on policy (e.g. Switzerland) display different patterns of participation from citizens living in countries in which state authority is centralized and where there are few opportunities for social movement organizations and other non-state actors to influence policy (e.g. France) (Císař & Vráblíková, 2012; Kriesi et al., 1995). In weak, decentralized states, there are higher levels of more moderate forms of action such as signing petitions and participating in campaigns, while in strong, centralized states there are higher levels of more extreme forms of action such as demonstrations and strikes. A relationship has also been found between the horizontal separation of power within the state (i.e. decentralization) and the overall level of citizen participation: The greater the separation of power, the higher the levels of participation (Vráblíková, 2013).

The *historical, economic, and cultural characteristics of countries* are also all related to patterns of both participation and engagement. For example, citizens in Eastern Europe tend to have lower levels of participation than those in Western Europe; however, in those countries where popular action contributed to the downfall of communist regimes, participation levels are higher (Bernhagen & Marsh, 2007). Women in more economically developed countries are more politically engaged and participate to a greater extent than those in less well-developed countries (Galligan, 2012), and women in countries which have predominantly Catholic traditions have lower levels of political interest, political knowledge, and political participation than women in countries which have predominantly Protestant traditions (Inglehart & Norris, 2003).

Finally, there are numerous macro contextual factors which are specifically related to patterns of participation by members of *minority and migrant groups*. These include whether or not such individuals are granted or denied voting rights, the rules for granting nationality and citizenship to foreign nationals in the country in which they are living, and the extent to which there are formal consultative bodies or channels for liaising with minority and migrant groups and for gathering advice on minority issues, interests, and concerns (Ireland, 1994; Martiniello, 2005; Penninx et al., 2004). Participation by minority individuals in community organizations and associations is also associated with higher levels of political participation (Fennema & Tillie, 1999; Putnam, 2000). Perceived discrimination and the context of reception provided by the majority society often function as precipitating factors which stimulate minority and migrant individuals into civic and political engagement and participation (Bedolla, 2000; Portes & Rumbaut, 2001, 2006; Rumbaut, 2008; Stepick, et al., 2008; Wray-Lake et al., 2008).

Demographic factors. Various demographic factors, including socioeconomic status (SES), ethnicity, migrant generational status, and gender, are also systematically linked to patterns of engagement and participation.

SES, in particular, is a major predictor. For example, individuals with higher SES have higher levels of political and civic knowledge (Delli Carpini & Keeter, 1996; Hart & Atkins, 2002; Niemi & Junn, 1998; Schulz et al., 2010) and higher levels of civic and political participation (Hart et al., 1998; Lopez & Marcelo, 2008; Zukin et al., 2006). However, it has been argued that what really matters as far as SES is concerned is the correlation between SES and educational attainment, and between SES and the skills that are acquired and exercised in organizations and in jobs, with the latter factors being the more direct determinants of participation (Verba et al., 1995; Wolfinger & Rosenstone, 1980).

Ethnicity is also associated with patterns of engagement and participation. For example, ethnic minorities and majorities participate in different kinds of volunteer activities, with the former participating more in activities relating to their own ethnic community and to other minorities (Jensen, 2010; Stepick et al., 2008). In addition, some minority youth are more likely to discuss news and world events with their parents than majority youth (Wray-Lake et al., 2008), although there are also findings suggesting that some minority youth are less likely than majority youth to have political and civic knowledge (Hart & Atkins, 2002; Torney-Purta et al., 2007). They may also be less likely than majority youth to express their political opinions (e.g. by contacting officials, expressing opinions to the media, and taking part in protests and petitions) (Zukin et al., 2006).

The *generational status* of migrant and minority individuals is also linked to patterns of participation (Seif, 2010). For example, the first generation is less likely to be registered to vote than later generations (Stepick et al., 2008), and is also less participative in terms of actual voting, volunteering, and boycotting when compared with majority group individuals (Lopez & Marcelo, 2008). By contrast, the second generation is often more civically and politically participative than majority group individuals (Lopez & Marcelo, 2008; Stepick & Stepick, 2002).

The relationships between ethnicity and political and civic participation are complex, involving multiple interactions between the specific ethnicity of the individual, gender, and types and levels of community participation (Bogard & Sherrod, 2008). Furthermore, it is arguable that many of the findings involving ethnicity are due to the reduced opportunities for participation that are linked to lower SES, lower educational attainment, and differential religious affiliations, rather than to ethnicity per se (Hart & Atkins, 2002; Verba et al., 1995).

Finally, as far as *gender* is concerned, gender differences have been found in political interest, voter turnout, legal and illegal political action, and participation in voluntary organizations (Galligan, 2012). Education and labour force participation are possible sources of these differences, with men being more likely to be highly educated and to have higher levels of employment than women, which means that they are more likely to acquire the necessary resources and social capital required for participation (Conway, 1999; Inglehart & Norris, 2003). That said, while men are more likely to have an interest in economic and foreign policy affairs, women are more engaged with social and environmental issues; Galligan (2012) argues that to understand these gendered patterns of participation, it is vital to also take into account the cultural, social, and religious norms that determine gender roles within a society, and the differential opportunities to engage that are made available to women and to men.

Social factors. Turning now to the proximal social factors that are related to civic and political engagement and participation, research has revealed that these are diverse and varied, with the sources of these factors being the family, education, the peer group, the workplace, the mass media, non-political organizations, and political institutions.

The *family* is linked in numerous ways to civic and political engagement and participation. For example: Literacy and educational resources in the family home predict levels of civic knowledge (Torney-Purta et al., 2001); adolescents whose parents are interested in political and social issues have higher levels of interest in these issues themselves as well as higher levels of civic knowledge (Schulz et al., 2010); a family ethic of social responsibility predicts levels of civic commitment (Flanagan et al., 1998); individuals whose parents engage in civic volunteering have higher levels of civic and political participation, are more attentive to news about politics and government, and are more likely to engage in consumer activism, while individuals who have frequent political discussions with family members are more likely to volunteer and to vote (Zukin et al., 2006);

the best predictor of political partisanship is parental political party preferences (Jennings & Niemi, 1968; Niemi & Jennings, 1991); parents who engage in protests are more likely to have offspring who also engage in protests (Jennings, 2002); and parents' levels of political knowledge predict their offsprings' levels of political knowledge, even into the latters' midlife (Jennings, 1996).

A further major source of influences on civic and political engagement and participation is *education* (Delli Carpini & Keeter, 1996; Emler & Frazer, 1999; Nie *et al.*, 1996; Niemi & Junn, 1998; Verba *et al.*, 1995; Zukin *et al.*, 2006). Some of the links here stem directly from the enhancement of the specific knowledge, skills, or motivations which are targeted by the school curriculum. For example, political knowledge can be increased through civics education if an appropriate pedagogical approach is adopted (Niemi & Junn, 1998), the emphasis which is placed upon elections and voting in school classes is a significant predictor of young people's intentions to vote in the future (Torney-Purta *et al.*, 2001), and the taking of school classes that generate an interest in politics and national issues predicts the likelihood of discussing the news and watching or listening to national news with parents (Chapman *et al.*, 1997).

However, the relationship between education and engagement and participation is much more wide ranging than just the specific knowledge, skills, or motivations targeted by the curriculum; educational effects generalize to a wide range of aspects of engagement and participatory behaviours. For example, Zukin *et al.* (2006) report that students who attend schools which provide civic training in skills (e.g. in letter writing and debating) are more likely to be involved in organizations outside school, to sign petitions, to participate in boycotts, to follow political news, to engage in charitable fundraising, and to attend community meetings. They also found that students who participate in classroom discussions about volunteering are more likely to volunteer regularly, to work on community problems, to participate in charity fundraising, and to try and influence other people's voting (see also Feldman *et al.*, 2007, and Pasek *et al.*, 2008, for similar findings).

Classroom climate also affects a wide range of engagement variables. For example, having an open classroom climate (i.e. the opportunity to discuss controversial social issues and to express and listen to differing opinions in the classroom) predicts young people's levels of civic knowledge and their likelihood of voting in the future (Torney-Purta *et al.*, 2001), levels of political interest and trust (Hahn, 1998), and the interpretation of political messages and internal efficacy (Azevedo & Menezes, 2007). Furthermore, perceptions that teachers practise a democratic ethic within the classroom predict the belief that one lives in a just society and levels of civic commitment (Flanagan *et al.*, 2007), transparency of teacher behaviour in the classroom predicts lower levels of political alienation (Gniewosz *et al.*, 2009), and participation in discussions within the classroom predicts internal efficacy (Ichilov, 1991).

However, education may actually have its most profound effects not through the enhancement of personal capacities and attitudes towards politics and civic activity. Nie *et al.* (1996) argue that it is the effects which education has upon individuals' employment opportunities, social networks, and positions of influence in later life that are critical, with these mediating factors being the actual drivers of people's patterns of participation in adult life.

Links have also been found between engagement and participation and the *peer group*. For example, civic participation is related to having positive relationships with peers (Wentzel & McNamara, 1999; Yates & Youniss, 1998), and there is evidence that when youth feel a sense of solidarity with peers at school and believe that most students in their school display institutional pride in the school, they are more likely to commit to civic and political goals and values (Flanagan et al., 1998). In addition, when youth believe that school, church, and college are important in their friends' lives and that they can discuss issues and problems with their friends, they are more likely to participate civically in later life (Zaff et al., 2008). However, the amount of time spent in the evenings outside the home with friends is inversely related to civic knowledge in countries where peer group culture devalues education (Torney-Purta, 2002; Torney-Purta et al., 2001).

Arrangements in the *workplace* are related to participation as well, with 'spillover' effects to political participation occurring from workplace arrangements that encourage democratic decision-making and the taking of responsibility (Almond & Verba, 1963; Greenberg et al., 1996; Kohn & Schooler, 1983; Mason, 1982). For example, having the authority to tell others what to do in the workplace and being involved in workplace decision-making predict the likelihood of voting, of being involved in campaigning for a political party or candidate, and of being involved in the affairs of one's local community (Guowei & Jeffres, 2008; Smith, 1996; Sobel, 1993).

The *mass media* can impact on engagement and participation. For example, the extent to which individuals attend to news reports on the television and in newspapers is related to levels of political and civic knowledge (Chaffee et al., 1970; Hahn, 1998; Linnenbrink & Anderman, 1995; Torney-Purta et al., 2001) and the likelihood of voting in the future (Torney-Purta et al., 2001). In addition, it has been found that people make decisions about whether to engage in consumer activism in response to information received from the news media and the Internet (Zukin et al., 2006). However, the total amount of television which is watched is inversely related to civic activism (Zukin et al., 2006).

Links have also been found between membership of *non-political organizations* and civic and political engagement and participation. For example, Hess and Torney (1967) found that membership of peer group organizations was linked to a greater political interest and an enhanced perception of government responsiveness in young people. More recently, it has been found that involvement in formal groups (e.g. religious groups, sports groups, etc.) in which the individual is able to take on active and specific roles is related to prosocial-oriented civic participation (Albanesi et al., 2007), young people who belong to a club or team are much more likely to be involved in community service two years later (Hart et al., 1998), people who have high levels of religious attendance and religious activity are more likely to be civically and politically active (Crystal & DeBell, 2002; Verba et al., 1995; Youniss et al., 1999; Zaff et al., 2008; Zukin et al., 2006), and young people who participate in community-based organizations and in extra-curricular activities are more likely to participate both civically and politically in later life (Glanville, 1999; Otto, 1975; Verba et al., 1995; Youniss et al., 1997; Zaff et al., 2003, 2008).

Finally, the activities of *political institutions* themselves are related to levels of participation. For example, being contacted and asked personally to participate in a civic or political process is a powerful predictor of later civic and political participation (Green & Gerber, 2004; Zukin et al., 2006). Mobilization by a political institution may be either direct (e.g. via street or doorstep campaigning, phone calls, mail shots, advertising, etc.) or indirect (where other people within an individual's social networks mobilize them into action) (Rosenstone & Hansen, 2003). Indirect mobilizing channels may be as effective as direct ones, especially when individuals live in decentralized states with a high number of independent veto points or power centres (Vráblíková, 2013).

Integrating existing findings on macro contextual, demographic, and social factors. The findings which have been reviewed so far are numerous and diverse, and it will be helpful to summarize these findings at this juncture. A diagrammatic summary is provided in Figure 1. This diagram shows the causal pathways through which macro contextual, demographic, and social factors can impact on political and civic engagement and participation.

Macro contextual factors are shown on the left-hand side of the diagram, and are categorized into two main types: (i) The specific characteristics of the electoral, political, and legal institutions and processes in the country in which an individual lives; and (ii) the broader characteristics of the country, including the historical, economic, cultural, and population characteristics of the country.

The demographic and social factors are shown in the centre of the diagram. It is clear from the preceding review that the beliefs, attitudes, values, norms, discourses, and practices of many different social actors can influence an individual's patterns of engagement and participation. Family discourses and practices play a particularly crucial role here, not only through their direct impact on the individual but also indirectly through, for example, parents' educational choices (which in turn influence the educational curriculum, teachers, and peer group to which their children are exposed) and through the purchase and use of

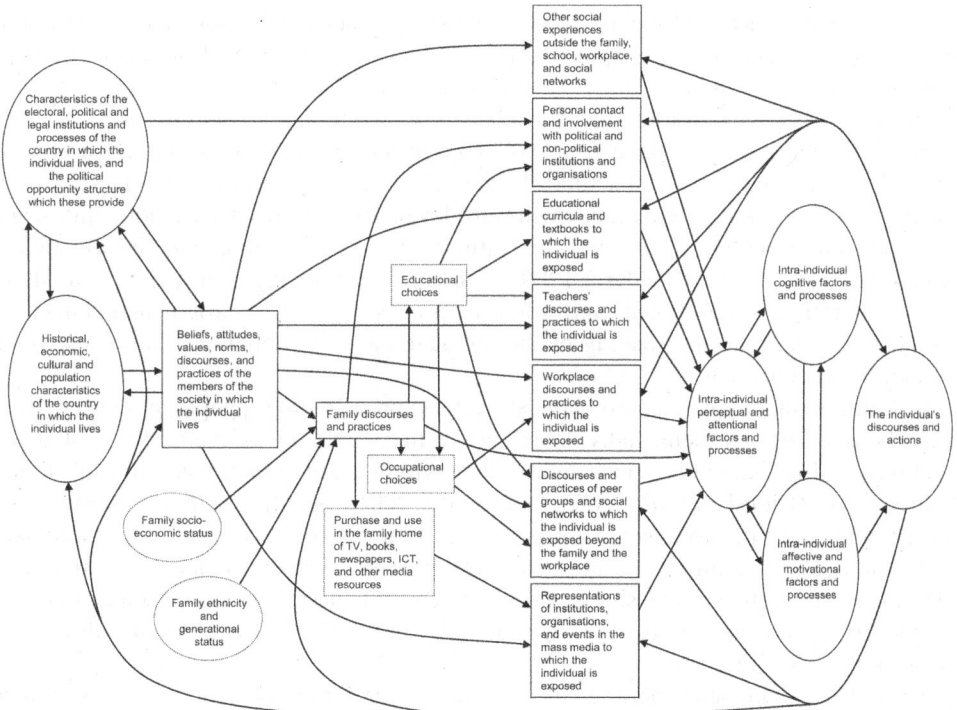

Figure 1. An integrative model of the macro and social factors driving political and civic participation and engagement (from Barrett, in press).

TV, books, newspapers, information and communications technology, and other media resources (which influences the media contents to which family members are exposed). Family discourses and practices themselves are, of course, heavily constrained and influenced by family SES, family ethnicity, and migrant generational status.

Psychological factors are shown in an abbreviated format on the right-hand side of the diagram. These factors are discussed more explicitly in the following section of this article.

The causal pathways through which macro contextual, demographic, and social factors influence an individual's patterns of engagement and participation are represented by the arrows in Figure 1. The two sets of macro factors mutually influence each other (institutional structures and processes influence the historical, economic, cultural, and population characteristics of countries, while these characteristics in turn influence institutional design and processes), and so there are bidirectional arrows between them. There are also bidirectional influences between both sets of macro factors and the beliefs, attitudes, values, norms, discourses, and practices of societal members (macro factors provide the setting against which individuals position themselves ideologically, politically, and socially, but individuals are also able to change the macro setting through their own political and civic actions).

Figure 1 summarizes how all of the following social factors can impact on an individual's political and civic engagement and participation: Family discourses and practices; educational curricula and textbooks; teachers' discourses and practices; workplace discourses and practices; discourses and practices of peer groups and social networks beyond the family and the workplace; other social experiences outside the family, the school, the workplace, and social networks; personal contact and involvement with political and non-political institutions and organizations; and representations of institutions, organizations and political and civic events in the mass media.

However, it is important to emphasize that these are all only *potential* sources of influence. Individuals do not passively absorb influences from their social environment. Instead, they are agentic social actors who actively select information from their environments, resist or ignore information which is irrelevant to their own needs, motivations, and goals, and construct their own beliefs and attitudes from the environmental information to which they have access (Bandura, 1986). In other words, endogenous perceptual, attentional, cognitive, motivational, and affective processes filter environmental influences and also contribute to the shaping of the political and civic beliefs and attitudes which an individual constructs.

In addition, individuals themselves have effects on how other people in their environment behave towards them. Individuals engage in interactions in many different social contexts, and the causality which takes place within these contexts is often inherently bidirectional (Kiousis *et al.*, 2005; McDevitt, 2006; Schaffer, 1996). Furthermore, where individuals rise to positions of power or influence within society, their discourses and actions can also impact on the macro characteristics of the society. The impact of the individual on the various social and macro contextual factors is depicted in Figure 1 by the arrows emanating from the individual's discourses and actions that flow from right to left in the diagram.

The balance of influence between the different factors varies from one societal setting to another, depending on the particular constellation of macro and social factors which is present. For this reason, different factors may be the primary drivers of political and civic engagement and participation in different demographic groups and in different settings, with the relative weightings assigned to the various arrows in Figure 1 varying from one societal setting to another and from one demographic group to another. This diagram therefore captures the variability which occurs across and within populations in the macro, demographic, and social factors that drive political and civic participation.

A more extended discussion of the model shown in Figure 1 is presented in Barrett (in press), which interested readers should consult for further details.

Psychological factors. In addition to the factors that have been discussed above, there are also many endogenous psychological factors that have been found to impact on civic and political participation. These factors together and cumulatively comprise what we have termed political and civic 'engagement' in this article.

First, a wide range of *cognitive factors* such as political and civic knowledge, beliefs, attitudes, opinions, and social and cultural values are linked to patterns of participation (Caprara *et al.*, 2006; Torney-Purta & Amadeo, 2003; Zukin *et al.*, 2006). For example, Zukin, *et al.* (2006) found that the most consistent predictor of all forms of participation was a factor which they termed 'political capital', which represents the total set of political resources that an individual has at the psychological level and includes political knowledge, the amount of attention paid to political issues, internal efficacy, and a sense of civic duty.

Other important cognitive factors that have been linked to participation are *social trust* (i.e. the belief that other people will generally behave in ways that are beneficial rather than detrimental to oneself), *institutional trust* (i.e. the belief that societal and political institutions will generally operate in ways that are beneficial rather than detrimental to people), and *beliefs about good citizenship* (Dalton, 2008; Norris, 1999; Putnam, 2000; Theiss-Morse, 1993). For example, Torney-Purta *et al.* (2004a; see also Torney-Purta *et al.*, 2004b) found that institutional trust predicted voting, volunteering, joining a political party, and writing letters to a newspaper about social or political concerns, while Theiss-Morse (1993) found that beliefs about good citizenship predicted voting, contacting government officials, other forms of conventional participation (e.g. persuading others how to vote), and non-conventional participation (e.g. joining public demonstrations).

Three specific cognitive factors that have been found to be particularly important are internal, external, and collective efficacy (Craig *et al.*, 1990; Klandermans, 1997; Pasek *et al.*, 2008; van Zomeren *et al.*, 2008). *Internal efficacy* (i.e. the belief that one understands civic and political affairs and has the competence to participate in civic and political events) is one of the most significant psychological predictors of participation, and it forms part of the cluster of beliefs that make up political capital (Zukin *et al.*, 2006). *External efficacy* (i.e. the belief that public and political officials and institutions are responsive to citizens' needs, actions, requests, and demands) also predicts participation. For example, half of the decline in electoral turnout in American presidential elections between 1960 and 1980 is attributable to the decline in external efficacy which took place across this period (Abramson & Aldrich, 1982). Both internal and external efficacy are related to political interest (Craig *et al.*, 1990; Schulz, 2005) and to institutional trust (Acock & Clarke, 1990). However, they have different patterns of relationships to other variables. For example, internal efficacy but not external efficacy is related to political knowledge (Delli Carpini & Keeter, 1996) and relationships between internal efficacy and participation are stronger and more consistent than relationships between external efficacy and participation (Craig *et al.*, 1990; Harris, 1999; Shingles, 1981). *Collective efficacy* (i.e. the belief that the problems of a group can be solved through collective activity) has been found to be especially important as a predictor of collective action (e.g. participating in protests and demonstrations), and is itself predicted by identification with the group and by the perception of social support for collective action within the group (Klandermans, 2002; van Zomeren et al., 2004, 2008).

Emotional factors are also related to civic and political participation. Both negative emotions (e.g. anger towards a perceived social injustice, feelings of discrimination, dissatisfaction with the status quo, and the desire to contribute to social change) and positive emotions (e.g. satisfaction with past participation experiences, institutional pride, and institutional trust) have been found to play a role (Flanagan et al., 1998; Leach et al., 2006; van Zomeren et al., 2004). For example, van Zomeren et al. (2004) found that levels of anger about a social or political issue directly predicts the likelihood of taking part in demonstrations and other forms of collective protest over that issue.

As noted already, *social identifications*, which involve experiencing a sense of belonging to a social group (such as a community, a social or political movement, an ethnic group, a national group, etc.), are linked to levels of participation (Deaux et al., 2006; Simon et al., 1998; van Zomeren et al., 2008). Social identifications entail adopting group norms concerning participation, and they can also provide in-group models for participatory behaviours and a sense of social support for one's opinions and actions. A somewhat broader psychological concept is that of *sense of community*, which consists of a number of psychological dimensions, including a feeling of being a part of a territorial or relational community, a feeling that one has opportunities for participation and influence within the community, a feeling that one's needs are being satisfied by the community, and a feeling of a shared emotional connection with other people within the community (McMillan & Chavis, 1986). A high sense of community predicts high levels of both political and civic participation (Cicognani & Zani, 2009).

Personal motivations and goals are also important. Motivations have been investigated most extensively in relationship to volunteering and civic participation (Omoto & Snyder, 1995, 2002), where it has been found that individuals have diverse motivations for participating in voluntary activities. These include: In order to express personal values; to acquire further knowledge and understanding; to gain experience and to develop personally; from a sense of community concern; and to enhance one's own self-esteem. The stronger these motivations are, the longer an individual engages in voluntary service (Omoto & Snyder, 1995).

Integrating existing findings on the psychological factors that comprise engagement. These numerous psychological factors interact with one another in complex ways. Individual psychological factors sometimes moderate or amplify the effects of other factors, and sometimes their effects on participation are mediated by other psychological factors rather than being direct. Explicit path models revealing the patterns of causality which operate between subsets of these psychological factors have been proposed by numerous researchers (Klandermans, 2002; Nie et al., 1996; Omoto & Snyder, 1995; Pasek et al., 2008; van Zomeren et al., 2004, 2008). These path models have focused primarily on the psychological engagement factors which predict three specific types of participation, namely collective action (e.g. participating in demonstrations), voting, and volunteering.

Interestingly, the individual path models which have been proposed can be connected together into a single much larger integrative model of the psychological factors comprising political and civic engagement, with no inconsistencies arising (Barrett, in press). This larger integrative model is shown in Figure 2, where single-headed arrows depict predictive relationships that have been identified through regression analyses or structural equation modelling, and double-headed arrows depict relationships that have been identified using correlations.

It is noteworthy that the model depicted in Figure 2 represents a single integrated causal psychological model of participation, with shared psychological factors across collective action, voting, and volunteering (in particular internal efficacy). This model provides a detailed specification of the perceptual, attentional, cognitive, affective, and motivational drivers of these three types of participation. It can therefore be viewed as an unpacking of these psychological components that are contained in the macro–demographic–social model shown in Figure 1. As such, this second model locks directly onto the previous model.

Connecting the two models together in this way produces a comprehensive integrative model of collective action, voting, and volunteering (which represent distinctive forms of non-conventional political, conventional political, and civic participation, respectively) which covers all four levels of factors: Macro, demographic, social, and psychological. The qualifications which were previously made in connection with Figure 1 also apply to this second model: That is, the factors and causal pathways which are shown in this model only denote *possible* factors and pathways. In practice, different subsets of

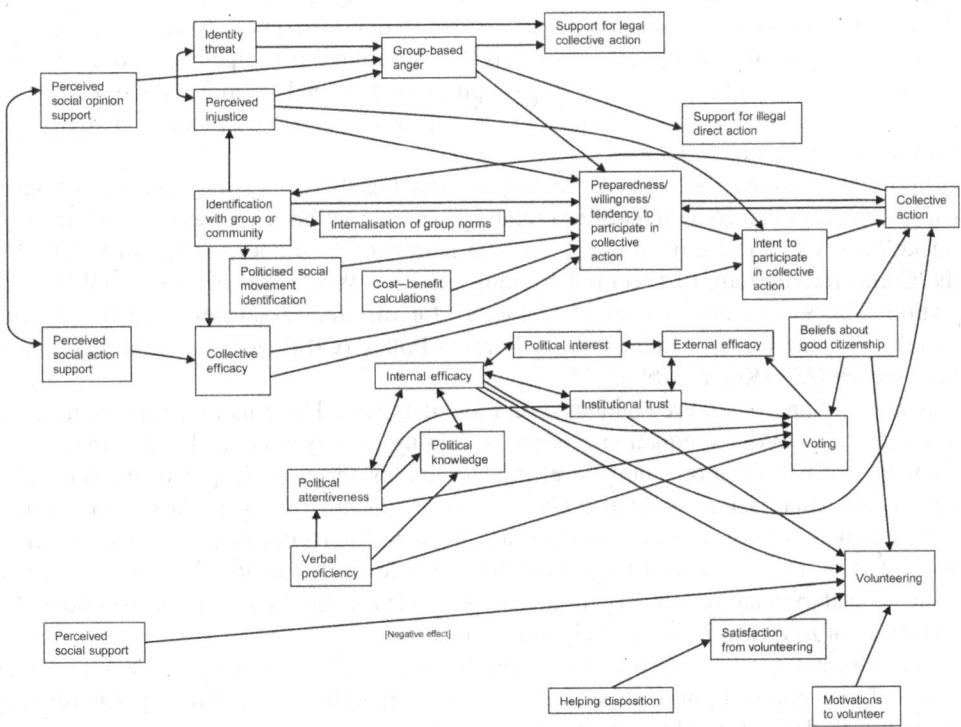

Figure 2. An integrative model of the psychological factors driving political and civic participation (from Barrett, in press).

factors and pathways will be the primary drivers of political and civic participation among different demographic subgroups and in different macro settings.

For further discussion of the model shown in Figure 2, interested readers should consult Barrett (in press).

A Summary of Some Findings Which Emerged from the Secondary Analysis of Existing Data-sets in the PIDOP Project

Rationale

We now turn to the second aim of this article, which is to provide a summary of some of the findings which emerged from the secondary analysis of existing data-sets in the PIDOP project. One way in which multiple levels of factors (such as those shown in Figures 1 and 2) can be explored simultaneously is through secondary analysis. There are many international survey data-sets which can be exploited for this purpose. One of the primary advantages of using the data from these surveys is the large sample sizes available, which permits powerful statistical modelling to be performed. A second advantage is that such surveys usually collect data from nationally representative samples, which boosts confidence in the results of the analyses.

The PIDOP project therefore undertook analyses of the data from several existing surveys (in addition to collecting new data in the nine participating countries). The overall aim of these secondary analyses was to identify empirically the factors which drive civic and political participation in different countries. There were two main sub-goals here: First, to describe patterns of civic and political participation across different countries and across key demographic groupings; and second, to identify the underlying factors which are related to variations in the patterns of civic and political participation both across and within countries.

In order to achieve these goals, the project drew together data from a number of international surveys that contain questions relating to participation. These were: The European Social Survey (ESS), Eurobarometer, the International Social Survey Programme (ISSP), the Comparative Study of Electoral Systems, and the World Values Survey (WVS). In addition, indices of macro contextual factors for different countries were taken from two sources, the Country Indicators for Foreign Policy (CIFP, 2011) and the Economist Intelligence Unit (Kekic, 2007).

A range of analyses were conducted on these data-sets. These included: Basic descriptive statistics; structural equation models examining the psychological and demographic predictors of participation; multi-level models linking these micro processes to broader macro contextual factors; and latent class analysis to identify distinct 'classes' of political participation. Because the data-sets do not include much information on the proximal social factors that are linked to participation, this level of factors was not included in these secondary analyses (but were instead addressed in the PIDOP project through the collection of new data in the participating countries).

Four distinct types of participation were examined in these analyses: Voting; other forms of conventional political participation (e.g. belonging to a political party, running for political election, working on political election campaigns for candidates or parties, giving donations to political parties, trying to persuade others to vote); non-conventional political participation (e.g. participating in protests, demonstrations and marches, signing petitions, writing letters or emails to politicians or public officials, writing articles or blogs with a political content for the media, and participating in fundraising events for a political cause); and civic participation (e.g. belonging to community organizations and other non-political organizations such as religious institutions, sports clubs, etc.).

A Summary of the Principal Findings

The descriptive analyses revealed that there was a great deal of variability in all four forms of participation, both within and across countries. However, some clear demographic consistencies across countries were also uncovered. For example: Younger people aged under 25 and ethnic minority individuals were less likely to vote in all countries; younger people were also less likely to be involved in conventional activities in all countries; and males were more likely to be involved in conventional forms of participation in all countries. In addition, in some but not all countries, younger people and ethnic minority individuals were more likely to be involved in non-conventional forms of political activity. As far as civic participation was concerned, there were also differences between countries, but there was comparatively less demographic variability within countries.

Analysis of Eurobarometer data collected since 1973 revealed consistently high *intentions* to vote each year (always above 80% of the sample). This was noticeably higher than the self-reported voting *behaviour* of individuals. It was also considerably higher than the actual levels of voter turnout in each country (which in some countries are as low as 50%). This demonstrates a disconnection between expressed voting intentions and actual behaviour.

Structural equation modelling was used to explore the relationships between psychological factors (i.e. engagement) and the four types of participation. These analyses were conducted on the data from the initial round of the ESS which fielded a series of questions covering 'Citizenship, Involvement, and Democracy'. Several psychological factors were investigated in these analyses, including:

- Attentiveness to political issues and affairs, for example, on television, on the radio, and in newspapers.
- Interest in politics.
- Internal efficacy.
- External efficacy.
- Institutional trust.
- Social capital—how much one trusts other people in general, and how often one meets with friends, relatives, or colleagues.
- Ideological identity—whether one holds an extreme position on either the right or the left of the political spectrum or whether one holds a more moderate centrist position.
- Opinionation—holding opinions about civic and political matters.
- Perceived discrimination—the perception that one is discriminated against because of the group to which one belongs.

A high degree of variability was found both across and within countries in these psychological factors. For example, levels of attentiveness and political interest vary widely across countries, from 20% of the population through to 65% depending on the country. However, some consistent patterns were overlaid on this variability. For example, attention to political broadcasts on television was always higher than attention to politics via other media sources, and there were lower levels of trust in politicians than in any other institution across all countries.

Consistent with the pathways shown in Figure 2, it was also found that people who had high levels of interest in politics and high levels of internal efficacy showed high levels of all four types of participation (i.e. voting, other forms of conventional political participation, non-conventional political participation, and civic participation). Such people were also more likely to hold opinions, with this high level of opinionation further increasing both their involvement in non-conventional political activities and their levels of civic participation. Opinionation has not previously been included in the psychological path models. Our findings suggest that it needs to be added to the model in Figure 2. In addition to being robust predictors of participation, political interest and internal efficacy were highly correlated with each other, so much so that in the statistical analyses their independent effects could not be isolated.

It was also found that perceived discrimination (an index of identity threat: See Figure 2) had different effects on different types of participation. For example, individuals who felt that they were discriminated against because of the group to which they belonged were less likely to vote, but were more likely to participate through other forms of conventional participation, non-conventional means, and civic means. The link between identity threat and collective action (a subtype of non-conventional political participation) is already represented in Figure 2 (mediated by group-based anger), but our findings suggest that identity threat also needs to be linked in the diagram to voting (negatively) and to volunteering (positively). It is a question for future research to address whether these links to voting and volunteering are similarly mediated by group-based anger or by other factors.

In addition, we found that high attentiveness to politics was linked to a greater tendency to vote and to participate civically, while high external efficacy increased the tendency to be involved in conventional and non-conventional activities, but showed no direct influence on voting behaviour. We also found that institutional trust was linked to a higher tendency to vote. All of these findings are consistent with Figure 2.

However, there were also some findings which were not consistent with the model shown in Figure 2. For example, while political attentiveness was indeed linked to both voting and civic participation (consistent with the model), political attentiveness was also *negatively* related to non-conventional political participation (inconsistent with the model, if collective action is viewed as a form of non-conventional participation). Further investigation is clearly required to elucidate the role of political attentiveness.

Multi-level modelling was used to examine the role of macro contextual factors. The main findings that were obtained are summarized in Table 2. The top rows in this table (labelled COUNTRY EFFECT) show the magnitude of country differences in each of the four forms of participation as revealed through the analysis of data from the ESS, the ISSP and the WVS. Significant differences between countries were found in all four forms of participation. The between-country differences were largest for civic participation (where 26% of the total variability in the ISSP, and 25% in the ESS, was due to between-country differences) and smallest for conventional participation (11% and 3%, respectively).

The central rows in Table 2 (labelled MACRO) show that, with the exception of voting, these between-country differences can be partially explained by differences in the macro contextual factors that characterize each country. A + in the table shows that there was a

Table 2. Results of the multi-level modelling (based on Brunton-Smith, 2011)

	Voting	Conventional participation	Non-conventional participation	Civic participation
		COUNTRY EFFECT		
ESS	7%	3%	17%	25%
ISSP		11%	22%	26%
WVS	19%			
		MACRO		
Democratic structures	NS	NS	+	+
Government efficiency	NS	+	+	+
Government accountability	NS	+	+	+
Human rights	NS	+	+	+
Political stability	NS	+	+	+
Rule of law	NS	+	+	+
		MACRO→MICRO		
Democratic structures	NS	NS	Gender[+], age[+], interest and efficacy[−]	Social trust[+]
Government efficiency	NS	Gender[+], age[+], interest and efficacy[−]	Gender[+], interest and efficacy[−]	Social trust[+]
Accountability	NS	Gender[+], interest and efficacy[−]	Gender[+]	Social trust[+]
Human rights	NS	Gender[+]	NS	Social trust[+]
Political stability	NS	Interest and efficacy[−]	Interest and efficacy[−]	Social trust[+]
Rule of law	NS	Gender[+], interest and efficacy[−]	Gender[+]	Social trust[+]

Notes: NS, Non-significant; +, higher score more likely to participate; −, higher score less likely to participate; [+], stronger effect; and [−], weaker effect.

statistically significant positive relationship between the macro factor and the form of participation, while NS shows that there was no significant relationship (NB no negative relationships were found). As can be seen, conventional political, non-conventional political, and civic participation were all positively related to macro factors. The strongest effects were associated with government efficiency, government accountability, and the country's record in relation to the rule of law (inclusion of these measures in the model accounted for well over half of the differences between countries). Participation levels were found to be higher in countries that were identified as performing well on these measures. The other macro factors were also linked to participation rates but were generally associated with smaller reductions in the variations attributable to between-country differences.

The lower rows in Table 2 (labelled MACRO → MICRO) summarize how differences in participation *within* countries are related to the macro characteristics of those countries. These rows show that the magnitude of differences in participation levels based on gender, levels of political interest, and internal efficacy (the latter two of which are strongly correlated with one another), and to a lesser extent age and social trust, are partially shaped by the macro factors characterizing the country in which the individuals are living. For example, in countries that are higher on government efficiency, the gender difference in levels of conventional and non-conventional participation is larger than average (represented by Gender[+] in the table); in countries that are lower on government efficiency, the gender gap in these forms of participation is smaller than average. The magnitude of gender differences in conventional and non-conventional forms of participation is also linked to government accountability and having a good record on the rule of law. In contrast, differences in conventional and non-conventional participation based on political interest and internal efficacy are *reduced* in countries which are high on government efficiency, government accountability, and a good record on the rule of law (represented by Interest and efficacy[−] in the table). The analyses also revealed that the positive role of social trust in generating civic participation is marginally more pronounced in countries which are high on all six macro factors.

Finally, latent class analysis was used to discover whether citizens can be grouped into different classes based on their patterns of participation. The analysis uncovered four distinct classes of people based on their overall pattern of participation:

- *Those who are both politically and civically active*—These individuals participate in all four ways to a high extent, and are more likely to be older, male, and not from an ethnic minority group.
- *Those who are inactive both politically and civically*—These individuals have a very low tendency to participate in all four ways, and are more likely to be younger and from ethnic minority groups, and are less likely to be male than those in the politically active group.
- *Those who have high levels of both non-conventional and civic activity*—These individuals are involved in non-conventional political activity and are civically engaged, but are less likely to vote or to be involved in conventional political activities. Compared to the politically and civically active group, this group is more likely to be young. Ethnic minority individuals are more likely to be in this third category than in the first category, but they are even more likely to be in the second, inactive, category above.
- *Voting-only*—These individuals are similar in demographic make-up to the politically and civically active group, but members are more likely to be female.

In summary, the analyses revealed that participation is indeed related to macro institutional factors, demographic factors, and psychological factors. There were significant variations between countries in the magnitude of some of the psychological drivers of participation, as well as differences within countries based on demographics. Importantly, the multi-level modelling revealed that the way that demographic factors (such as gender and age) and psychological factors (such as political interest, internal efficacy, and social trust) relate to forms of participation other than voting is influenced by macro factors (especially government efficiency, government accountability, and the rule of law).

The existence of these complex patterns demonstrates the need for theoretical explanations to encompass macro, demographic, and psychological drivers of political and civic participation. The findings also demonstrate the need for theoretical explanations to address the specificities of particular types of participation (voting, other forms of conventional political participation, non-conventional political participation, and civic participation) among particular demographic subgroups living within particular national contexts. Thus, the outcomes of these analyses underline the need for integrative multi-level theories of participation, rather than theories that focus on only a single level of factors.

Readers wishing to find out more about the details of the secondary analyses which were conducted under the PIDOP project, and the findings that were obtained, should consult Brunton-Smith (2011), which provides a full technical report of all the analyses that have been summarized in this section.

Conclusion

It is clear from the previous research reviewed in the first part of this article and from the secondary analyses reported in the second part that civic and political participation are influenced by multiple levels of factors, including distal macro contextual factors, demographic factors, proximal social factors,[2] and endogenous psychological factors (i.e. psychological engagement). In addition, it is clear that the factors that operate at these different levels interact in complex ways in driving citizens' patterns of participation.

Two psychological factors which were identified as having a consistent effect on all four types of participation (i.e. voting, other forms of conventional political participation, non-conventional participation, and civic participation) were political interest and internal efficacy. This finding suggests that psychological interventions aimed at increasing levels of participation should focus primarily on amplifying the political interest and internal efficacy of the individuals that are being targeted. For example, in the case of youth, the programmes that are adopted by schools or youth centres should aim at encouraging young people in developing an interest in political and civic affairs, fostering their knowledge and understanding of political and civic matters, and supporting their acquisition of the personal skills which they require in order to participate effectively in the political and civic life of their community and country.

However, the finding that factors at different levels interact in driving patterns of participation implies that policies or interventions targeting psychological factors other than political interest and internal efficacy may have to be tailored specifically to particular demographic subgroups living within particular national contexts. In other words, different policies or forms of intervention may be required in different national contexts and for enhancing participation among younger vs. older individuals, women vs. men, and minority vs. majority individuals.[3]

The findings from the PIDOP project also present a challenge for social scientists' attempts to explain the nature and causes of political and civic participation in theoretical terms. As factors at all four levels clearly do have an influence on participatory behaviours, theoretical explanations that fail to incorporate all four levels in their formulations will inevitably be only partial. Similarly, theories which fail to take into account that factors at different levels interact to drive citizens' patterns of participation will likewise be limited in their explanatory power. Instead, integrative multi-level theories which take into account the specific psychological characteristics and social circumstances of particular demographic subgroups living within particular national contexts (such as the one that has been presented across Figures 1 and 2 in this article) are required. The further elaboration of such theories is likely to require substantial collaboration between political scientists, sociologists, and psychologists.

Acknowledgements

The research reported in this article was supported by a grant received from the European Commission's 7th Framework Programme, FP7-SSH-2007-1, Grant Agreement no: 225282, *Processes Influencing Democratic Ownership and Participation (PIDOP)*.

Notes

1. Full details of the project are available on the PIDOP project website at http://www.fahs.surrey.ac.uk/pidop/.
2. Although proximal social factors were not included within the secondary analyses reported here, their influence was confirmed in the PIDOP project by the new data collected in the participating countries.
3. For full information about the implications of the findings of the PIDOP project for policy, practice, and intervention, interested readers should consult the PIDOP Policy Recommendations document which may be accessed at http://www.fahs.surrey.ac.uk/pidop/Recommendations.htm.

References

Abramson, P. R. & Aldrich, J. H. (1982) The decline of electoral participation in America, *American Political Science Review*, 76(3), pp. 502–521.
Acock, A. C. & Clarke, H. D. (1990) Alternative measures of political efficacy: Models and means, *Quality and Quantity*, 24(1), pp. 87–105.
Albanesi, C., Cicognani, E. & Zani, B. (2007) Sense of community, civic engagement and social well-being in Italian adolescents, *Journal of Community and Applied Social Psychology*, 17(5), pp. 387–406.
Almond, G. & Verba, S. (1963) *The Civic Culture: Political Attitudes and Democracy in Five Nations* (Princeton, NJ: Princeton University Press).
Azevedo, C. N. & Menezes, I. (2007) Learning politics beyond cognition: The role of experience and participation in political development, in: N. Kryger & B. Ravn (Eds) *Learning Beyond Cognition*, pp. 95–114 (Copenhagen: Danish University of Education).
Bandura, A. (1986) *Social Foundations of Thought and Action* (Englewood Cliffs, NJ: Prentice-Hall).
Barrett, M. (in press) An integrative model of political and civic participation: Linking the macro, social and psychological levels of explanation, in: M. Barrett & B. Zani (Eds), *Political and Civic Engagement: Multidisciplinary Perspectives* (London: Routledge).
Bedolla, L. G. (2000) They and we: Identity, gender and politics among Latino youth in Los Angeles, *Social Science Quarterly*, 81(1), pp. 106–122.
Bernhagen, P. & Marsh, M. (2007) Voting and protesting: Explaining citizen participation in old and new European democracies, *Democratization*, 14(1), pp. 44–72.
Bobo, L. & Gilliam, F. D. (1990) Race, sociopolitical participation and black empowerment, *American Political Science Review*, 84(1), pp. 377–393.
Bogard, K. L. & Sherrod, L. R. (2008) Citizenship attitudes and allegiances in diverse youth, *Cultural Diversity and Ethnic Minority Psychology*, 14(4), pp. 286–296.
Brunton-Smith, I. (2011) *Modelling Existing Survey Data*, Full Technical Report of PIDOP Work Package 5, Department of Sociology, University of Surrey. Available at http://epubs.surrey.ac.uk/739988/ (accessed 29 June 2012).
Caldeira, G. A., Patterson, S. C. & Markko, G. A. (1985) The mobilisation of voters in congressional elections, *Journal of Politics*, 48(2), pp. 490–509.
Caprara, G. V., Schwartz, S., Capanna, C., Vecchione, M. & Barbaranelli, C. (2006) Personality and politics: Values, trait and political choice, *Political Psychology*, 28(5), pp. 609–632.
Chaffee, S. H., Ward, L. S. & Tipton, L. P. (1970) Mass communication and political socialization, *Journalism Quarterly*, 47(4), pp. 447–459.

Chapman, C., Nolin, M. J. & Kline, K. (1997) *Student Interest in National News and Its Relation to School Courses* (NCES 97-970) (Washington, DC: National Center for Education Statistics).

Cicognani, E. & Zani, B. (2009) Sense of community and social participation among adolescents and young adults living in Italy, in: D. Dolejšiová & M. A. Garcia López (Eds) *European Citizenship—In the Process of Construction: Challenges for Citizenship, Citizenship Education and Democratic Practice in Europe*, pp. 100–113 (Strasbourg: Council of Europe Publishing).

CIFP (2011) *Country Indicators for Foreign Policy: Governance and Democracy Processes* (Ottowa: Carleton University).

Císař, O. & Vráblíková, K. (2012) Contextual determinants of political participation. Unpublished paper, Work Package 3, The PIDOP Project.

Conway, M. M. (1999) *Political Participation in the United States*, 3rd edn (Washington, DC: CQ Press).

Craig, S. C., Niemi, R. G. & Silver, G. E. (1990) Political efficacy and trust: A report on the NES pilot study items, *Political Behaviour*, 12(3), pp. 289–314.

Crystal, D. S. & DeBell, M. (2002) Sources of civic orientation among American youth: Trust, religious valuation, and attributions of responsibility, *Political Psychology*, 23(1), pp. 113–132.

Dalton, R. J. (2008) *The Good Citizen: How a Younger Generation is Reshaping American Politics* (Washington, DC: CQ Press).

Deaux, K., Reid, A., Martin, D. & Bikmen, N. (2006) Ideologies of diversity and inequality: Predicting collective action in groups varying in ethnicity and immigrant status, *Political Psychology*, 27(1), pp. 123–146.

Delli Carpini, M. & Keeter, S. (1996) *What Americans Know about Politics and Why It Matters* (New Haven, CT: Yale University Press).

Emler, N. & Frazer, E. (1999) Politics: The education effect. *Oxford Review of Education*, 25(1–2), pp. 251–274.

Feldman, L., Pasek, J., Romer, D. & Jamieson, K. H. (2007) Identifying best practices in civic education: Lessons from the student voices program, *American Journal of Education*, 114(1), pp. 75–100.

Fennema, M. & Tillie, J. (1999) Political participation and political trust in Amsterdam: Civic communities and ethnic networks, *Journal of Ethnic and Migration Studies*, 25(4), pp. 703–726.

Flanagan, C. A., Bowes, J. M., Jonsson, B., Csapo, B. & Sheblanova, E. (1998) Ties that bind: Correlates of adolescents' civic commitments in seven countries, *Journal of Social Issues*, 54(3), pp. 457–475.

Flanagan, C., Cumsille, P., Gill, S. & Gallay, L. (2007) School and community climates and civic commitments: Patterns for ethnic minority and majority students, *Journal of Educational Psychology*, 99(2), pp. 421–431.

Galligan, Y. (2012) *The contextual and individual determinants of women's civic engagement and political participation*. Unpublished paper, Work Package 3, The PIDOP Project.

Geys, B. (2006) Explaining voter turnout: A review of aggregate-level research, *Electoral Studies*, 25(4), pp. 637–663.

Glanville, J. L. (1999) Political socialization or selection? Adolescent extracurricular participation and political activity in early adulthood, *Social Science Quarterly*, 80(2), pp. 279–290.

Gniewosz, B., Noack, P. & Buhl, M. (2009) Political alienation in adolescence: Associations with parental role models, parenting styles and classroom climate, *International Journal of Behavioral Development*, 33(4), pp. 337–346.

Green, D. P. & Gerber, A. S. (2004) *Get Out the Vote! How to Increase Voter Turnout* (Washington, DC: Brookings Institution Press).

Greenberg, E. S., Grunberg, L. & Daniel, K. (1996) Industrial work and political participation: Beyond 'simple spillover', *Political Research Quarterly*, 49(2), pp. 305–330.

Guowei, J. & Jeffres, L. (2008) Spanning the boundaries of work: Workplace participation, political efficacy, and political involvement, *Communication Studies*, 59(1), pp. 35–50.

Hahn, C. (1998) *Becoming Political: Comparative Perspectives on Citizenship Education* (Albany, NY: State University of New York Press).

Harris, F. C. (1999) Will the circle be unbroken? The erosion and transformation of African–American civic life, in: R. Fullinwider (Ed.) *Civil Society, Democracy and Civic Renewal*, pp. 317–338 (New York: Roman and Littlefield).

Hart, D., & Atkins, R. (2002) Civic development in urban youth, *Applied Developmental Science*, 6(4), pp. 227–236.

Hart, D., Atkins, R. & Ford, D. (1998) Urban America as a context for the development of moral identity in adolescence, *Journal of Social Issues*, 54(3), pp. 513–530.

Hess, R. D. & Torney, J. V. (1967) *The Development of Political Attitudes in Children* (Chicago, IL: Aldine).

Highton, B. & Wolfinger, R. E. (1998) Estimating the effects of the National Voter Registration Act of 1993, *Political Behavior*, 20(2), pp. 79–104.

Ichilov, O. (1991) Political socialization and schooling effects among Israeli adolescents, *Comparative Education Review*, 35(3), pp. 430–447.

Inglehart, R. & Norris, P. (2003) *Rising Tide: Gender Equality and Cultural Change Around the World* (Cambridge: Cambridge University Press).

Ireland, P. (1994) *The Policy Challenge of Ethnic Diversity* (Cambridge, MA: Harvard University Press).

Jackman, R. W. (1987) Political institutions and voter turnout in the industrial democracies. *American Political Science Review*, 81(2), pp. 405–423.

Jackman, R. & Miller, R. A. (1995) Voter turnout in the industrial democracies during the 1980s. *Comparative Political Studies*, 27(4), pp. 467–492.

Jennings, M. K. (1996) Political knowledge over time and across generations, *Political Opinion Quarterly*, 60(2), pp. 228–252.

Jennings, M. K. (2002) Generation units and the student protest movement in the United States: An intra- and intergenerational analysis, *Political Psychology*, 23(2), pp. 303–324.

Jennings, M. K. & Niemi, R. G. (1968) The transmission of political values from parent to child. *American Political Science Review*, 62(2), pp. 169–184.

Jensen, L. A. (2010) Immigrant youth in the United States: Coming of age in diverse cultures, in: L. R. Sherrod, J. Torney-Purta & C. A. Flanagan (Eds) *Handbook of Research on Civic Engagement in Youth*, pp. 425–443 (Hoboken, NJ: John Wiley & Sons).

Kekic, L. (2007) *The Economist Intelligence Unit's Index of Democracy. The World in 2007* (London: The Economist).

Kiousis, S., McDevitt, M. & Wu, X. (2005) The genesis of civic awareness: Agenda-setting in political socialization, *Journal of Communication*, 55(4), pp. 756–774.

Klandermans, B. (1997) *The Social Psychology of Protest* (Oxford: Blackwell).

Klandermans, B. (2002) How group identity helps to overcome the dilemma of collective action, *American Behavioral Scientist*, 45(5), pp. 887–900.

Kohn, M. & Schooler, C. (1983) *Work and Personality: An Inquiry into the Impact of Social Stratification* (Norwood, NJ: Ablex).

Kriesi, H., Koopmans, R., Duyvendak, J. W. & Giugni, M. G. (1995) *New Social Movements in Western Europe: A Comparative Analysis* (London: UCL Press).

Leach, C. W., Iyer, A. & Pedersen, A. (2006) Anger and guilt about ingroup advantage explain the willingness for political action, *Personality and Social Psychology Bulletin*, 32(9), pp. 1232–1245.

Linnenbrink, L. & Anderman, E. M. (1995) Motivation and news-seeking behaviour. Paper presented at the Annual Meeting of the American Educational Research Association, San Francisco, CA, 18–22 April.

Lopez, M. H. & Marcelo, K. B. (2008) The civic engagement of immigrant youth: New evidence from the 2006 Civic and Political Health of the Nation Survey, *Applied Developmental Science*, 12(2), pp. 66–73.

Martiniello, M. (2005) Political participation, mobilisation and representation of immigrants and their offspring in Europe. *Willy Brandt Series of Working Papers in International Migration and Ethnic Relations*, 1/05, Malmö University, Malmö, Sweden.

Mason, R. (1982) *Participatory and Workplace Democracy* (Carbondale, IL: Southern Illinois University Press).

Mattila, M. (2003) Why bother? Determinants of turnout in the European elections, *Electoral Studies*, 22(3), pp. 449–468.

McDevitt, M. (2006) The partisan child: Developmental provocation as a model of political socialization, *International Journal of Public Opinion Research*, 18(1), pp. 67–88.

McMillan, W. D. & Chavis, M. D. (1986) Sense of community: A definition and a theory, *Journal of Community Psychology*, 14(1), pp. 6–23.

Nie, N. H., Junn, J. & Stehlik-Barry, K. (1996) *Education and Democratic Citizenship in America* (Chicago, IL: University of Chicago Press).

Niemi, R. G. & Jennings, M. K. (1991) Issues and inheritance in the formation of party identification, *American Journal of Political Science*, 35(4), pp. 970–988.

Niemi, R. & Junn, J. (1998) *Civic Education: What Makes Students Learn?* (New Haven, CT: Yale University Press).

Norris, P. (Ed.) (1999) *Critical Citizens: Global Support for Democratic Governance* (Oxford: Oxford University Press).

Oberholzer-Gee, F. & Waldfogel, J. (2001) Electoral acceleration: The effect of minority population on minority voter turnout. *NBER Working Paper 8252*, National Bureau of Economic Research, Cambridge MA.

Omoto, A. M. & Snyder, M. (1995) Sustained helping without obligation: Motivation, longevity of service, and perceived attitude change among AIDS volunteers, *Journal of Personality and Social Psychology*, 68(4), pp. 671–686.

Omoto, A. M. & Snyder, M. (2002) Considerations of community: The context and process of volunteerism, *American Behavioral Scientist*, 45(5), pp. 846–867.

Otto, L. B. (1975) Extracurricular activities in the educational attainment process, *Rural Sociology*, 40(2), pp. 162–176.

Pasek, J., Feldman, L., Romer, D. & Jamieson, K. H. (2008) Schools as incubators of democratic participation: Building long-term political efficacy with civic education, *Applied Developmental Science*, 12(1), pp. 26–37.

Penninx, R., Martiniello, M. & Vertovec, S. (Eds) (2004) *Citizenship in European Cities: Immigrants, Local Politics and Integration Policies* (London: Ashgate).

Portes, A. & Rumbaut, R. G. (2001) *Legacies: The Story of the Immigrant Second Generation* (Berkeley, CA: University of California Press).

Portes, A. & Rumbaut, R. G. (2006) *Immigrant America: A Portrait*, 3rd edn (Berkeley, CA: University of California Press).

Powell, G. B. (1986) American voter turnout in comparative perspective, *American Political Science Review*, 80(1), pp. 17–43.

Putnam, R. D. (2000) *Bowling Alone: The Collapse and Revival of American Community* (New York: Simon & Schuster).

Rosenstone, S. J. & Hansen, J. M. (2003) *Mobilization, Participation, and Democracy in America* (New York: Longman).

Rumbaut, R. G. (2008) Reaping what you sew: Immigration, youth, and reactive ethnicity, *Applied Developmental Science*, 12(2), pp. 108–111.

Schaffer, H. R. (1996) *Social Development* (Oxford: Blackwell Publishers).

Schulz, W. (2005) Political efficacy and expected participation among lower and upper secondary students. A comparative analysis with data from the IEA Civic Education Study. Paper presented at the European Consortium for Political Research General Conference, Budapest, 8–10 September.

Schulz, W., Ainley, J., Fraillon, J., Kerr, D. & Losito, B. (2010) *Initial Findings from the IEA International Civic and Citizenship Education Study* (Amsterdam: IEA).

Seif, H. (2010) The civic life of Latina/o immigrant youth: Challenging boundaries and creating safe spaces, in: L. R. Sherrod, J. Torney-Purta & C.A. Flanagan (Eds) *Handbook of Research on Civic Engagement in Youth*, pp. 445–470 (Hoboken, NJ: John Wiley & Sons).

Shingles, R. D. (1981) Black consciousness and political participation: The missing link, *American Political Science Review*, 75(1), pp. 76–91.

Simon, B., Loewy, M., Sturmer, S., Weber, U., Freytag, P., Habig, C., Kampmeier, C. & Spahlinger, P. (1998) Collective identification and social movement participation, *Journal of Personality and Social Psychology*, 74(3), pp. 646–658.

Smith, V. (1996) Employee involvement, involved employees: Participative work arrangements in a white-collar service occupation. *Social Problems*, 43(2), pp. 166–179.

Smith, E. S. (1999) The effects of investments in the social capital of youth on political and civic behaviour in young adulthood: A longitudinal analysis, *Political Psychology*, 20(3), pp. 553–580.

Sobel, R. (1993) From occupational involvement to political participation: An exploratory analysis, *Political Behavior*, 15(4), pp. 339–353.

Stepick, A. & Stepick, C. D. (2002) Becoming American, constructing ethnicity: Immigrant youth and civic engagement, *Applied Developmental Science*, 6(4), pp. 246–257.

Stepick, A., Stepick, C. D. & Labissiere, Y. (2008) South Florida's immigrant youth and civic engagement: Major engagement: Minor differences, *Applied Developmental Science*, 12(2), pp. 57–65.

Theiss-Morse, E. (1993) Conceptualizations of good citizenship and political participation, *Political Behavior*, 15(4), pp. 355–380.

Torney-Purta, J. (2002) The school's role in developing civic engagement: A study of adolescents in twenty-eight countries, *Applied Developmental Science*, 6(4), pp. 203–212.

Torney-Purta, J. & Amadeo, J.-A. (2003) A cross-national analysis of political and civic involvement among adolescents, *PS: Political Science & Politics*, 36(2), pp. 269–274.

Torney-Purta, J., Barber, C. H. & Richardson, W. K. (2004a) Trust in government-related institutions and political engagement among adolescents in six countries, *Acta Politica*, 39(4), pp. 380–406.

Torney-Purta, J., Richardson, W. K. & Barber, C. H. (2004b) Trust in government-related institutions and civic engagement among adolescents: Analysis of five countries from the IEA Civic Education Study. *CIRCLE Working Paper 17*, University of Maryland, Centre for Information and Research on Civic Learning and Engagement (CIRCLE).

Torney-Purta, J., Barber, C. H. & Wilkenfeld, B. (2007) Latino adolescents' civic development in the United States: Research results from the IEA Civic Education Study, *Journal of Youth and Adolescence*, 36(2), pp. 111–125.

Torney-Purta, J., Lehmann, R., Oswald, H. & Schulz, W. (2001) *Citizenship and Education in Twenty-Eight Countries: Civic Knowledge and Engagement at Age Fourteen* (Amsterdam: IEA).

Verba, S., Schlozman, K. L. & Brady, H. E. (1995) *Voice and Equality: Civic Volunteerism in American Politics* (Cambridge, MA: Harvard University Press).

Vertovec, S. (2009) *Transnationalism* (London: Routledge).

Vráblíková, K. (2013) How context matters? Mobilization, political opportunity structures, and nonelectoral political participation in old and new democracies, *Comparative Political Studies* doi: 10.1177/0010414013488538

Wentzel, K. R. & McNamara, C. C. (1999) Interpersonal relationships, emotional distress and prosocial behaviour in middle school, *Journal of Early Adolescence*, 19(1), pp. 114–125.

Wolfinger, R. E. & Rosenstone, S. J. (1980) *Who Votes?* (New Haven, CT: Yale University Press).

Wray-Lake, L., Syvertsen, A. K. & Flanagan, C. A. (2008) Contested citizenship and social exclusion: Adolescent Arab American immigrants' views of the social contract, *Applied Developmental Science*, 12(2), pp. 84–92.

Yates, M. & Youniss, J. (1998) Community service and political identity development in adolescence, *Journal of Social Issues*, 54(3), pp. 495–512.

Youniss, J., McLellan, J., Su, A., & Yates, M. (1999) The role of community service in identity development: Normative, unconventional, and deviant orientations, *Journal of Adolescent Research*, 14(2), pp. 248–261.

Youniss, J., McLellan, J. A. & Yates, M. (1997) What we know about engendering civic identity, *American Behavioral Scientist*, 40(5), pp. 620–631.

Zaff, J. F., Malanchuk, O. & Eccles, J. S. (2008) Predicting positive citizenship from adolescence to young adulthood: The effects of a civic context, *Applied Developmental Science*, 12(1), pp. 38–53.

Zaff, J. F., Moore, K. A., Papillo, A. R. & Williams, S. (2003) Implications of extracurricular activity participation during adolescence on positive outcomes, *Journal of Adolescent Research*, 18(6), pp. 599–630.

van Zomeren, M., Postmes, T. & Spears, R. (2008) Toward an integrative social identity model of collective action: A quantitative research synthesis of three socio-psychological perspectives, *Psychological Bulletin*, 134(4), pp. 504–535.

van Zomeren, M., Spears, R., Fischer, A. & Leach, C. W. (2004) Put your money where your mouth is! Explaining collective action tendencies through group-based anger and group efficacy, *Journal of Personality and Social Psychology*, 87(5), pp. 649–664.

Zukin, C., Keeter, S., Andolina, M., Jenkins, K. & Delli Carpini, M. X. (2006) *A New Engagement? Political Participation, Civic Life, and the Changing American Citizen* (New York: Oxford University Press).

Participation, Dialogue, and Civic Engagement: Understanding the Role of Organized Civil Society in Promoting Active Citizenship in the European Union

CRISTIANO BEE & ROBERTA GUERRINA

School of Politics, University of Surrey, Guildford, UK

ABSTRACT *This article looks at current policies concerning the civic and political participation of youths, women, migrants, and minorities in the European Union. It highlights the ways in which active citizenship and civic engagement have become a political priority for European institutions. Representation of local policy actors at the supranational level and strategies for the inclusion of civil society provide a platform for evaluating the impact of Europeanization at the national and subnational level. The article focuses on key discourses and narratives associated with specific policy frames (e.g. European citizenship, European social policies, and the European public sphere (EPS)). Some of the key questions addressed by the article are: What are the strategies that are employed, both by the European institutions in Brussels and organized civil society (OCS), to enhance participation and reciprocal communication? What vision of governance do practices such as active engagement and civil dialogue represent? Drawing on current theories of governance, our article contributes to the debate about the EPS by evaluating the role of OCS in bridging the gap between European institutions and national polities. Equally, our focus on traditionally marginal groups provides a platform for assessing the institutionalization of the 'European social dimension'.*

Introduction

This article draws on the work of a project looking at Processes Influencing Democratic Ownership and Participation (PIDOP) in Europe, sponsored by the European Commission's 7th Framework Programme. In particular, it presents some of the findings from policy analysis that looked at the civic and political participation of youths, women, migrants, and minorities in Europe. The article reflects upon the most recent attempts of the European Union (EU) to reinvigorate the basis of participatory democracy at every level of European governance. Our central argument is that active citizenship has become an increasingly central area of policy for European institutions as a vehicle for facilitating the development of a European public sphere (EPS). Our main aim here is to outline the drivers of this process and unpack the factors that—at the level of the EU—have determined this shift in political discourse. The article draws on policy analysis to explain the emergence of this new political discourse at the European level between 2005 and 2010.

The democratic crisis triggered by the rejection of the European Constitutional Treaty in 2005 provided an opportunity to make active citizenship a concrete policy area/objective (Kingdon, 2011). Despite the criticisms of the European Commission's efforts to reinvigorate the democratic basis of the EU, the 2005 initiative led by Margot Wallström, Vice President of the European Commission for Institutional Relations and Communication Strategy under the first Barroso presidency (2004–2010), is worthy of notice. Her approach is based on a wide set of programmes (e.g. Plan D for Democracy, Dialogue and Debate) aimed at promoting a citizens' orientated form of European integration (Commission of the European Community—CEC, 2005). This strategy is prevalent in institutional discourse and was recently introduced in the Treaty on the Functioning of the EU under Article 11 of Lisbon. It seeks to establish a wider basis for the participation and engagement of stakeholders' networks, non-governmental organizations (NGOs), and the activists that form the core of European civil society. Issues such as active citizenship, representation of local policy actors at the supranational level, strategies for civic engagement, and empowerment of civil society organizations become benchmarks for evaluating the impact of Europeanization at the national and local level. It is worth noting that these principles are also at the heart of 'Europe 2020', a political strategy based upon advocacy and network building.

This article explores some of the challenges entrenched in the study of civil society engagement and interest representation in Europe. Our analysis is first and foremost interested in understanding the interaction between dominant policy discourses (coming mainly from, e.g. the European institutions and policy actors) and the emergence of counter-narratives (from, e.g. civil society organizations) at the national and European level. The approach adopted by this article is discursive in nature, but it is also sensitive to the importance of content and context. We locate our discussion of the development of organized civil society (OCS) in Europe within the context of current debates about democratic accountability and the establishment of an EPS. Positioned at the interface between national and European politics, civil society organizations play a key role in promoting political engagement. The increased interest in OCS at the European level also indicates recognition of the role these organizations play in promoting the project within national communities. The analysis presented in the empirical section of this article highlights strengths and weaknesses of this political strategy for enhancing democratic ownership of the European project. The development of active citizenship—both as a coherent policy area and as a vehicle for increasing the engagement of traditionally marginal groups—provides useful insights into institutional strategies for dealing with the crisis of Europe and the rise of popular opposition to the European project.

Our article thus looks at four issues: (1) institutional and non-institutional strategies for enhancing participation and reciprocal communication; (2) plans for enhancing the reach of these strategies; (3) implications of active engagement and civil dialogue for democratic governance in Europe; and (4) opportunities and constraints entrenched in these practices.

Understanding Civic Engagement and Participation: Methodological Considerations

Our approach to policy analysis produces a form of policy tracing, not dissimilar to the work conducted by the MAGEEQ[1] project (Verloo, 2005). We are foremost concerned with how values and norms play a role in the construction of the agenda and the mechanisms for involving different institutional and non-institutional policy actors. We developed a model of discourse analysis that integrates insights from post-structuralism as well as critical discourse analysis. In regard to the former, we looked at the importance of power relations in framing the interactions between various policy actors and their competition to shape meaning on specific policy concepts that become discursive nodal points (DNPs). In regard to the latter, we looked at the importance of political context in shaping DNPs, and in orientating the political strategies of public institutions.

The development of a networked territorial space is a consequence of the current processes of transnationalization. Social constructivists have claimed that it was necessary to find ways to unpack the EU's transformative effect on social realities (Christiansen *et al.*, 1999). This can be achieved by looking at the dynamics and discursive interactions between constellations of strong, transnational, and weak publics. These networks contribute to the transformation of identities, cognitive schemas, and structures of meanings for individuals. In turn, this process does not entail a passive adaptation to the forces of Europeanization, but instead interacts with conflictual and fragmented structures.

Discourse analysis is increasingly being adopted by social scientists as a useful tool for understanding the complexities of social and political structures (Diez, 2001; Dryzek, 2008; Howart & Torfing, 2005). This approach looks at the role of language and communications in shaping the social world and, in turn, influencing the formulation of social policies. As Hajer (2002) argued, '[D]iscourse is defined as an ensemble of ideas, concepts, and categories through which meaning is given to phenomena. Meaning is thus produced and reproduced through an identifiable set of practices' (p. 63). For the purpose of this article, discourse analysis is a useful tool as it looks at the interaction between different publics, the reciprocal dynamics of power, and the establishment of specific argumentative strategies formulated to impose a certain meaning on social reality (Liebert, 2007).

There is a growing body of literature on governance that is gradually replacing 'state-centric' approaches to public policy analysis. These new approaches take into account new sites, actors, and themes in the development of key policies and their objectives. In referring to Castells' thinking on the network society, Hajer and Wagenaar (2003) emphasize a shift in the language from 'institutions to networks', underlining the complexity of policy-making which is increasingly framed by a wide set of competing social actors vying for a voice in the public arena. In these terms, discursive approaches require an understanding of the structures of power and systems of meaning prevailing at the different levels of the EU as a system of governance (Ingram & Schneider, 2008). This approach is particularly useful for the analysis presented here as it allows us to assess how institutional and non-institutional discourses compete to shape meaning of European democratic governance.

A central question in discourse analysis is therefore the issue of power. Unpacking how power is articulated and manipulated is essential to understand the following: first, who imposes specific meanings on social realities; and second, who participates (or not) in framing public discourses. In fact, different, and often competing, discourses are articulated at the same time, challenging each other and often overlapping each other. From the position of the policy analyst, discourse analysis aims to understand why particular meanings become dominant and authoritative, whilst others are discredited. Diez (2001) refers to Europe as a 'discursive battleground', to represent the idea of the different and simultaneous struggles for shaping meaning on public discourses related to key concepts such as governance, citizenship, public sphere, identity, etc. From his position, DNPs are 'central concepts in the political debate around which meaning is stabilized' (Diez, 2001, p. 16), whose meanings are fixed by a set of discursive practices and meta-narratives through articulation (Laclau & Mouffe, 1985).

As Figure 1 shows, DNPs are defined in our approach by a combination of variables such as context, policy priorities, and meta-narratives. We argue that active citizenship as a European Commission-sponsored policy is introduced into the agenda because of the combination of four DNPs: (1) democratization and public sphere; (2) Europeanization and transnationalization; (3) political participation and civil dialogue; and (4) European social dimension. The discursive bargaining that takes place between a number of institutional and non-institutional actors in order to shape meaning—thus the DNPs—provides useful insights on convergence as well as fragmentation in the agenda-setting mechanisms at the EU level. We argue that this process is best explained by focusing our discussion on the development of the EPS and the role played by civil society organizations in its constitution.

European Identity, Civil Society, and Public Communication Management: Constructing the Public Sphere

The normative debate about the EPS concentrates on whether this is a feasible reality at the European level. There is agreement in the literature that the existence of a public sphere is important because it entails discussion, interaction, and the development of discourses on questions of public concern (Eriksen & Fossum, 2000, 2002). It is a social construct that

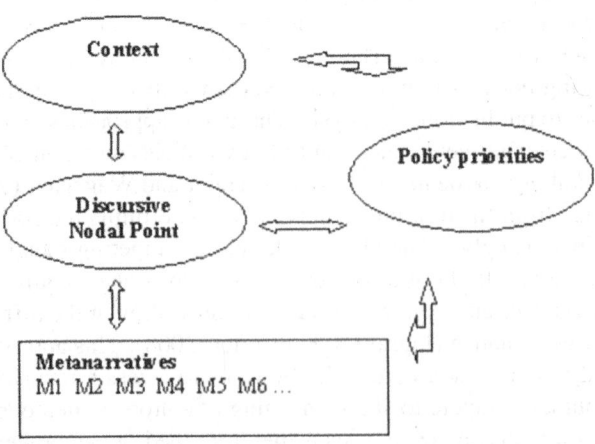

Figure 1. Discursive nodal point.

drives democratization and at the same time, as some critics of the Habermasian model (1989) argued (see for instance Fraser, 1992, 1995), entails confrontation and fragmentation between dominant discourses and counter-discourses produced by different social actors, such as ethnic minorities (Schulz-Forberg, 2010).

According to Calhoun (2003), the development of a 'properly' EPS is important because it enhances the base for participatory democracy, something seen as necessary to address broader issues of democratic deficit and legitimacy (Bellamy & Castiglione, 2000; Kohler-Koch & Rittberger, 2007). The absence of a truly *EPS* is thus considered to reflect a lack of public support for the project as a whole. It is perhaps worth underlining here that the debate on the development of the EPS ran parallel to the famous confrontation between Habermas (1995) and Grimm (1995) that generated a new body of scholarship looking at the development of a transnational public sphere. More specifically, it looks at issues such as the Europeanization of the media, political communication, and the framing of European public opinion (Díez-Medrano, 2003; Statham, 2007; Trenz, 2010).

It is also worth noting the potential impact of a European political space on shaping the social imaginary, which results from improving dialogic communicative practices in the EU. As a result of this process and 'sponsorship', the European imagined community is to be conceived of as a top-down—and elite-centred/driven—construction (Guerrina, 2002; Shore, 2000). It is not by chance that policy-makers and eurocrats have concentrated on identifying agents of European consciousness; these are the actors that will advance/promote the development of the EPS and European identity more generally (Bee, 2010).

The process of constructing a European identity therefore requires the establishment of a social imaginary linked to a sense of Europeanness. A key requirement for the success of this process is the establishment of awareness-raising mechanisms designed to highlight the benefits of the European integration process. European institutions funded a range of programmes aimed at developing transnational social spaces with a European dimension, thus hoping to develop the collective imaginary required for the construction of a common identity. It is worth remembering the large set of EU-funded initiatives that enhance ties between different groups or collectivities (e.g. cities, regions, and municipalities) in the fields of cultural, educational, and social policies. Research on European cities of culture has highlighted how transforming urban spaces can influence the development of a transnational reality with clear European connotations (Sassatelli, 2009).

The main concern of this debate revolves around the social dimension of the European project. Clearly, civil society has a key role to play in fostering the development of a sense of solidarity at the European level. Calhoun (2002) understands the public sphere as a form of social solidarity, which is discursively produced and reproduced by the exchange between citizens and institutions. Pivotal in this process is the ability to foster the development of a social imaginary based on a shared sense of belonging to a territorial, cultural, and political space. Key actors in this process are non-state actors promoting equality and social inclusion at the European level (Ruzza, 2004). It is in this context that we can see how the development of a 'properly' EPS is essential for mutual recognition and social cohesion.

Clearly this debate provides the backdrop against which European policy actors—both institutional and non-institutional—can maximize opportunities for influencing the policy process. In this context, questions about feasibility and 'reproducibility' of state-centric models of public sphere have become more poignant (Harrison & Wessels, 2009; Schlesinger, 1999; Van de Steeg, 2002). The absence of a common media, shared language, and shared political culture works against the establishment of a homogenous EPS. The presence of wide-reaching interest representation at the European level through an eclectic civil society is often seen as a disadvantage (Bellamy, 2010; Scharpf, 1998). Focusing predominantly on the national polity as the locus of citizenship practice, these arguments neglect, or dismiss, the existence of a pan-EPS. Eriksen (2004) accepts that a nationally bound public sphere is no longer feasible, but argues that 'the European public space is currently fragmented, differentiated and in flux' (p. 18).

Policy networks, new social media, and civil society organizations are drivers in the constitution of a networked public sphere based on discursive interactions. By the very nature of the actors involved, these interactions are taking place at different levels of European governance. They have different capacity for influence and exchange at the European level; however, they come together to give meaning to a European social reality in what Diez (2001) calls the 'European Discursive Battleground'.

The development of a system of networked governance is shaped by the process of Europeanization that allows for transnational interactions and exchange. What emerges is a complex picture, not like Castells' (1996) vision that the EU is a networked society, but more closely aligned with Schlesinger and Kevin's (2000, pp. 217–218) model of multilevel governance. They claim that a better—more realistic—way of applying the concept of public sphere to the EU is by taking into account the interactions of the multiple publics and actors at work within this transnational polity. Schlesinger (2003) goes on to explain how these different actors and polities act inside the European communicative space. He deduces that this space is increasingly constituted by networks in which different actors interact and exchange information (cf. Koopmans & Pfetsch, 2003; Trenz & Eder, 2004). The interaction—often competition—between transnational and national interests shapes how power is allocated in the development of the EPS. The institutional structure of the EU reinforces the development of strong and weak publics that are often oriented towards representing the interest of national polities (Schlesinger, 2003, p. 1). In this context, the EU could be understood to be a body charged with the development of a social communication platform designed to connect different spheres and polities (Schlesinger, 2003, p. 4). As it will be shown in the rest of this article, this process is not linear but implies the production of fragmented and often opposing discourses. Civil society organizations have a significant role to play in helping European institutions in the process of identity building. Through this process they become the vehicle through which the EPS is created—thus contributing to the dissemination of the dominant, institutionally based discourse—as well as being the actors responsible for the formulation of counter-narratives.

Actors in the EPS: The Role of the OCS

The extensive body of literature on European civil society concentrates on institutional dynamics and structures. Of particular interest to the analysis presented here are those projects looking at political socialization and institutional cultures (Warleigh, 2001) and the Europeanization of civil society (Ruzza & Bozzini, 2008). The interplay between institutional and non-institutional actors at the European level has also been of particular interest to scholars looking at the changing nature and role of civil society in Europe. The analysis of lobbying practices in and towards Brussels is particularly useful in understanding the context within which OCS operates (Coen, 2007; Greenwood, 2007; Sánchez-Salgado, 2007).

OCS can be defined as that group of non-state actors which have a direct and formalized relationship with European institutions. It includes NGOs, social movements, advocacy groups, charities, representatives of self-help organizations, and promotional groups (Ruzza, 2004). The power of these organizations has grown considerably in the networked system, that is, the EU (Kohler-Koch & Rittberger, 2007; Smismans, 2006), where power is dispersed along different nodes and governance structures that are no longer bounded by state sovereignty (Warleigh, 2001).

This process, however, has generated two competing spheres. On the one hand, there are highly institutionalized civil society organizations that work within formal structures and networks as discussed above. On the other hand, a number of critical forces, such as social movements, have started to emerge. These new social actors use the EPS in a way that is more fluid and non-institutionally bound. It is the latter group that is increasingly responsible for producing a critique of Europeanization (Della Porta, 2009). The development of transnational protest and interactive practices in arenas such as the European Social Forum are prime examples of civil society organizations producing counter-narratives and alternatives to institutional practices (Balme & Chabanet, 2008). The distinction between types of civil society organization is important here because it helps us to understand how they facilitate—or not—the establishment of a European polity. If we assume that OCS is key to the development of the EPS, then understanding its interaction—however complex—with institutional structures is essential to explain how it facilitates ownership and engagement amongst traditionally marginal groups.

More specifically, by conceptualizing the fragmentation of the EPS in networks, discourses, and spheres of publics we can look at distinct claims about how interests are represented at different levels of European governance. The asymmetrical influence also exercised by different groups over policy-making processes also helps us to understand how power manifests itself within network governance. As we have already established the EPS is a top-down, elite-driven process; it is thus worth remembering that, over time the EU has sought to address such concerns by developing an approach to public communication that involves social actors (such as the civil society and the media) as well the general public.

The White Paper on Communication (CEC, 2006) and Plan D (CEC, 2005) represent a critical junction for the way European institutions manage this process. Firstly, these policies enhanced the EU's capacity to communicate about transnational issues. Secondly, and perhaps more importantly, they also transformed public campaigning from an activity into a public policy. They sanctioned a formal budget for this policy area and defined specific priorities and spheres of intervention. We can easily find examples of how these policies have been implemented by looking at the main EU communication campaigns of the last five years, e.g. social communication on 'sensitive issues', like health, global warming, the environment, anti-discrimination, and gender equality. At the same time, European institutions have also sought out the involvement of non-state actors in the development and execution of the actual campaigns. This model is known in public communication theory as the 'symmetrical model of public relations' (Fawkes, 2004; Grunig & Grunig, 1992). In a nutshell, it is based on the enhancement of mutual, interactive, and dialogic relationships between institutional and non-institutional actors in constructing the public discourse on issues of public interest.

It is worth noting that institutional communication is a public relations activity and a way of producing public communication. It can be defined as a set of activities organized by institutional actors on questions of public concern, which entails several closely aligned elements. Firstly, institutions have an agenda-setting role to play in as far as they need to decide what needs to be communicated. Secondly, the institutions need to enable interaction between citizens and policy-makers. Thirdly, there have to be opportunities for feedback on policy proposal interventions organized by public bodies. Finally, citizens have to be able to influence and change institutional activities throughout the feedback process. The basic assumption that underpins this process is that a fully democratic political system must find a way to develop open and accessible communication tools.

Figure 2 illustrates the interactions between public institutions, citizens, and 'mediators' in what is a bidirectional model of communication (Mancini, 2003). Public institutions produce outputs on questions of public concern that target sectors of public opinion and/or specific target groups. In this model, communication is achieved through the exchange between citizens and public institutions whereby the citizens—or specific targets groups—contribute by providing input to the process in order to redirect or stabilize public policies. The discursive battleground is located at the interface between institutionally sponsored public information campaigns—i.e. top-down—and citizens/civil society—i.e. bottom-up—responses to the policy process. This model implies some

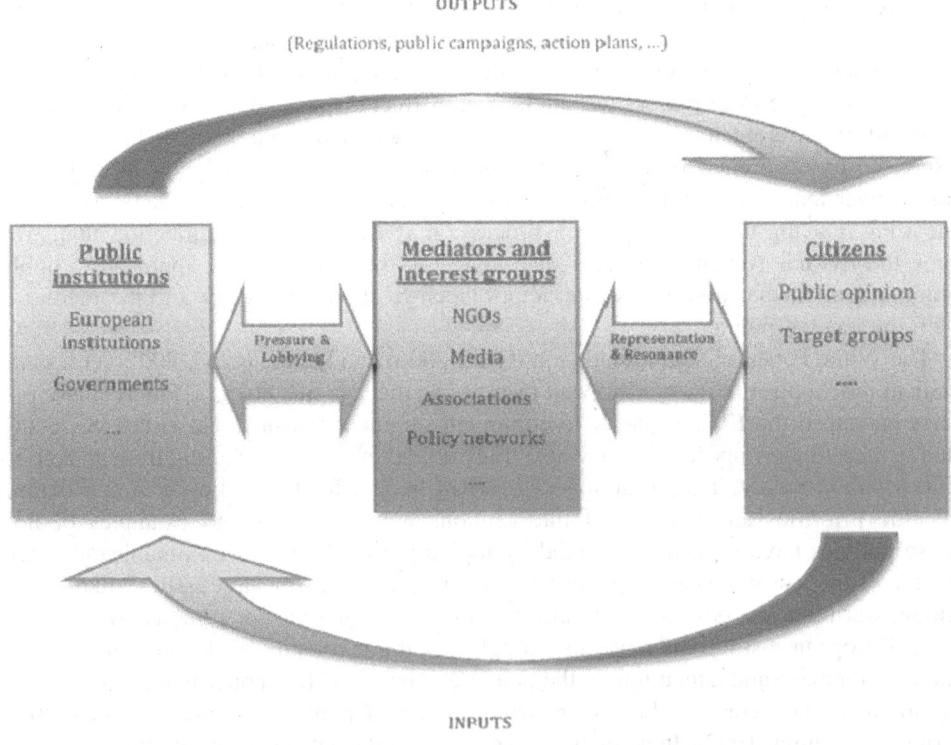

Figure 2. The model of bidirectional institutional communication.

kind of discursive encounter or struggle to legitimize the process. As such, it is most effective when bottom-up inputs reach policy-makers, thus signalling participation and representation. The model therefore hinges upon the ability of the 'mediators'—i.e. civil society organizations—to engage with the public institutions; the pressure they levy on these public institutions and the way they represent citizens' interests ultimately shape the scope and reach of the final policy outcomes. The idea of active citizenship becomes particularly relevant in this discussion in as far as it allows citizens to engage directly with policy-makers, and without the intervention of mediators, for the pursuit of a common interest. Our article focuses specifically on the bottom-up responses to official policy documents and public information campaigns. It therefore looks at the effectiveness of OCS as a moderator in the process and a vehicle for citizens' participation and representation.

The work carried out by the PIDOP project, particularly in the context of understanding current policy approaches to improving political participation and engagement, shows that application of this ideal model of institutional communication at the European level is challenged by various factors, above all, the complexity of European governance, the dispersion of power between different levels, and the existence of strong, transnational, and weak publics. These variables ultimately contribute to the creation of multiple polities with unbalanced access to European institutions. Our analysis shows that the development of a mutual, transparent, symmetrical, and bidirectional model of institutional communication favours interactions between strong and transnational publics, at the expense of weak public spheres. Awareness of the biases at the heart of European communication policy and its application to active citizenship therefore calls for a detailed analysis of the impact these processes have on the establishment of active citizenship at the European level.

Active Citizenship in the EU: Unpacking the Discourse

The PIDOP project focused on key policy development in the area of active citizenship and participation at the European level between 2004 and 2010. We have been particularly interested in how these policy trends shaped the political agenda of the European Commission and how OCS responded to institutional efforts to increase political participation and representation of traditionally marginal groups.

The EU has always been a magnet for a wide range of civil society organizations seeking to lobby and influence European institutions. The very nature of European governance encouraged the participation of OCS in a supranational setting. Umbrella organizations—e.g. Social Platform, CONCORD, the European Youth Forum (EYF), and the European Women's Lobby (EWL)—act as catalyst for the engagement of a wide range of social interests at the European level. They have a privileged position in the Brussels arena and thus they are an example of a strong public looking to represent the interests of transnational organizations connected with them. However, questions need to be asked about their own accountability and how effective they are at representing weaker publics such as NGOs, associations, and organizations that operate at the subnational levels. Concentration of power and access in the hand of strong transnational umbrella organizations ultimately reduces the opportunities for weaker groups to influence public policies and to make their voices heard at the European level. This asymmetrical structure challenges a core assumption at the heart of European approaches to active citizenship, i.e. that OCS can and/or should act as legitimizing force for the EU.

This section will unpack this complex set of interactions, thus contributing to current debates about governance, legitimacy, and democracy in Europe. The section will focus on European OCS in an attempt to assess how the extent to which these groups have become institutionalized and therefore agents of European political communication, as opposed to active representatives of a counter-discourse.

Our analysis concentrates on the range, scope, and depth of interactions between OCS and the European Commission in order to uncover these organizations' influence on the development of the European policy agenda. In order to account for the asymmetrical development of structures for active citizenship, we selected a number of policy documents produced by the European Commission in the period 2004–2010. The large number of public campaigns initiated by the Commission in the period between 2004 and 2010 is a direct consequence of Plan D and the White Paper on Communication Policy. These campaigns are particularly relevant for the PIDOP project because of their focus on minority rights, social exclusion, anti-discrimination, poverty, intercultural dialogue, equality, and similar topics. The intention is to unpack the direction of travel or trajectory of European strategies for civil society engagement during the Barroso I presidency. In keeping with the focus of the PIDOP project, we concentrated on three categories of citizens (i.e. youth, women, migrants, and minorities). Four DNPs emerged from the wider European political context and the analysis of these documents. These DNPs are significant for our discussion as they frame European institutional discourse on political participation and civic engagement. The next step in our research was to select and analyse an equal number of policy documents produced by supranational umbrella civil society organizations, e.g. the EYF, the EWL, the Social Platform, CONCORD, EurActiv, European Network Against Racism (ENAR), and Solidar.[2]

Our sample was then examined to assess the development of policy narratives around the concept of active citizenship, which is the main analytical frame for this article. The analysis to follow therefore looks at the development of active citizenship, as it is linked to four key DNPs (Table 1). The article thus sets out how active citizenship was introduced as a policy objective and how it relates to specific policy actions (e.g. policy programmes such as Youth in Action or legislative instruments such as Art. 11 of the Lisbon Treaty).

Table 1. Emerging discourses and policy development

Processes (DNPs)	Policy outcomes
Democratization and public sphere	Plan D (Dialogue, Democracy, Debate)
Europeanization and transnationalization	Europe 2020
Political participation	Key funding and networking in areas such as youth policy, gender equality, and integration policy
European social dimension	Art. 11 Lisbon Treaty: Youth in Action
	Art. 13 Amsterdam Treaty: European Years, Hague programme, Road Map, etc.

Four DNPs emerge as dominant, each supported by various meta-narratives—e.g. European identity, future Europe, and Euro crisis. The specific political context that characterized European integration between 2004 and 2010—e.g. the rejection of the Constitutional Treaty, enlargement, the ratification of the Lisbon Treaty, the publication of Europe 2020, etc.—defines these narratives and discourses by promoting specific political priorities, such as the development of an open and transparent EU based on the participation of civil society. The rest of this article will look at how OCS responded to institutional discourses on active citizenship and whether it was successful in advancing a counter-discourse. The analysis is particularly insightful as it provides evidence of the range and scope of critiques advanced by umbrella organizations in Brussels. The focus of these counter-discourses is specific policy initiatives aimed at improving active citizenship and civic engagement. Overall, it traces how the DNPs become sites of contestation for non-state actors. When taken together the meta-narratives produced by the OCS in relation to the DNPs challenge dominant discourses on active citizenship proposed by the European Commission.

Democratization and Public Sphere

The European Commission's response to the rejection of the Constitutional Treaty in 2005 indicates institutional recognition of the need to improve the democratic foundations of the European project. From this point the Commission makes a concerted effort to enhance the basis of participatory democracy at the European level by increasing opportunities for interaction and exchange with the 'public'. This approach is also an attempt to develop a bidirectional model of public communication that feeds into the Commission's understanding of public sphere and governance.

It is important to unpack the Commission's strategy for dealing with one of the most significant challenges faced by the EU: popular rejection of the project. In response to the challenge laid down by emerging social forces, the Commission put forward a number of meta-narratives aimed at 'fixing' those dimensions of the EPS deemed to be undermining key institutional objectives. It adopted a set of argumentative strategies aimed at imposing a dominant discourse on the EPS. This process allows the Commission to take ownership of the concept—so that it becomes the EU's public sphere—thus stabilizing its meaning. This top-down process of construction of meaning is challenged by a wide set of counterpublics that generate meta-narratives that challenge the very notion of an EU-dominated EPS. The productive exchange between institutional—i.e. dominant—narratives and non-institutional discourses can be seen as a battle to establish meaning.

From this perspective the EPS is fluid and subject to discursive mediation, i.e. its meaning is not fixed and the subject will only stabilize when another dominant discourse emerges. It is worth noting that European civil society has widely challenged the notion of the public sphere proposed by the European Commission. Cited below is an example of counter-discourse offered by EurActiv (2006) after the publication of Plan D (CEC, 2005). EurActiv's (2006) Plan D: Diversify, Decentralise, Disseminate, Decide, challenges the Commission's vision of a homogeneous public sphere. In particular, EurActiv's (2006) argues for the establishment of a networked and decentralized approach:

> The European public sphere is certainly desirable, given what some call the federalist vocation of the EU. But is it achievable within a reasonable time? (...)

> Rather, are there not multiple public spheres, fragmented by national and socio-professional canters of interest? If so, one should privilege interconnection of national spheres/benchmarking (...) rather than trying to create one European public sphere. (p. 5)

The interpretation of this 'struggle' to impose meaning on the concept of public sphere has to be understood in light of two other DNPs: (1) Europeanization and transnationalization and (2) political participation. EurActiv's position focuses on diffusion of leadership and power as a route to promote democratic governance at the European level.

EurActiv's meta-narrative is driven by an overarching aim to account for the role of transnationalization in the construction of the EPS. This position is intended to challenge the definition of the EU's public sphere as defined—or fixed—by the European Commission. In order to resist the discursive underpinning of the official narrative (DNP), EurActiv's articulation of a counter-discourse must be accompanied by specific mechanisms (e.g. civil dialogue) that guarantee open interplay (i.e. public communication) between institutional and non-institutional actors. It is worth noting here that the European Commission has substantially increased the opportunities for civil organizations to provide input into the policy-making process. Open consultations on public policies are now fairly common practice and have greatly enhanced the ability of 'counterpublics' to influence and change the meaning of a DNP (Bozzini, 2007). There are two defining features to this process of engagement that ultimately impact upon the quality of interest representation at the European level. Firstly, consultation is now an intrinsic part of the EU's communication strategy. Secondly, official communications and consultations are largely directed at strong and transnational publics.

Debates about the most appropriate ways of communicating to marginal groups in order to enhance ownership and participation at the European level is a recurrent concern of many policy documents we analysed. This process of contestation highlights the OCS's perceived ambiguity in the development of the EPS. It also points to an increased fragmentation and contestation of the vision put forward by the European Commission.

Despite increased recognition that the EU can be a catalyst for change in social matters, there is also a sense that it has to compete with other—perhaps more powerful—sources of information. Take for instance the representation of minority groups in the media; European public discourse on equality and diversity is in direct competition with sources of information that are more accessible by the public. The limited reach of the EPS and its competition with national political narratives ultimately undermine the effectiveness of European policy initiatives. The ENAR's (2008) assessment of EU project to fight racism highlights this tension:

> Many ethnic and religious minority groups have been affected by public perception and the negative debate on migration. The negative portrayal of migration by policy makers and by the mass media through stereotypical language and negative images has led to a worrying increase in racism and xenophobia towards third country nationals. (p. 1)

In this extract, ENAR identifies public representation of minorities by the media and some sections of the political sphere as one of the drivers for social exclusion and discrimination in Europe. The organization considers it to foster stereotypes of the strong public sphere (i.e. the majority groups) towards the weak one (i.e. minorities). On this account the organization in fact remarks that

> The media continues to have a major influence on the perceptions of minority communities. [...] The conspicuous lack of minority representation in all forms of media also creates a misperception, especially when the only representation is negative stories and stereotypes. News stories will often identify the ethnicity or origin of those perpetrators who are foreign or belong to a minority community, in contrast to when a member of the majority population commits a crime. (ENAR, 2010, p. 12)

Together these extracts highlight some of the recurring themes associated with current debates about transparency and accountability at the European level. They also stress the challenges entrenched within an asymmetrical communication structure whereby European public institutions are reliant on member states and civil society organizations for dissemination and engagement. Lack of a European media and/or meaningful engagement with transnational issues is the main problem for the establishment of a European political space. On this account, we can thus underline the emergence of a number of challenging issues that are put forward by the OCS in answer to the European Commission's project to shape the EPS.

Europeanization and Transnationalization

Focusing on European-level discourse highlights the increasing centrality of the processes of Europeanization and transnationalization. The relationship between national and European NGOs is a recurrent theme that emerges from the analysis of civil society documents. The asymmetrical relationship between these two levels and the ability of the latter to represent the interest of national groups has been a central point of discussion. Weaker groups' exclusion from strong European networks reduces their capacity to influence public policies. The power of European-level OCS to act as gatekeeper needs to be recognized, if issues of legitimacy and representation are to be addressed in a meaningful way. This consideration is true of all OCS, but it is particularly important in relation to traditionally marginal groups as it defines the parameters for membership.

The process of Europeanization is not linear. Rather, it is fragmented both vertically (EU to member states) and horizontally (member state to member state). The way that this process affects civil society organizations is interesting because it highlights the complex web of interactions and tensions at the heart of European governance.

Civil society organizations thus serve a dual function. They are both a source of legitimacy for institutional meta-narratives, as well as the main source of opposition to dominant discourses. The organizations included in our analytical sample accept the values, policy objectives, and political priorities identified by European institutions. In this context, they therefore legitimize the four DNPs emerging at the European level. At the same time, they distance themselves from the Commission's narratives by not engaging with the objectives of specific European programmes or core principles relative to the European integration process. It is interesting to note that reference to core policy meta-narratives addressed at the supranational level (e.g. constitutionalism or identity) rarely make an appearance.

The European Commission's attempts to bring civil organizations 'into the fold' are increasingly the object of reflection and critique. For example, in December 2008, Social Platform launched an annual conference on *Civil dialogue—how can we shape the Europe we want?* Hard to reach communities across Europe were the subject of much debate. Empowerment, improvement of information flows at the local level, enhancement of education, and opportunities for communities are some of the key tasks transnational NGOs agreed to take on (Social Platform, 2008). This response sought to address concerns about the inclusiveness and representation of European-level civil society organizations. It is also a good example of the bottom-up dynamics started by grassroots organizations to demand better representation in policy processes.

The socio-economic conditions of specific groups influence access to power and decision-making mechanisms. This is true at the national level, but it is an even more poignant consideration when thinking about European governance. The complexity of European processes increases the distance between policy actors and citizens. This is particularly true of traditionally marginal groups that rely on civil society organizations for interest representation and access to political institutions. The EYF's narrative reflects these concerns. When looking at the integration of 'young people with fewer opportunities', the Forum points to the extent to which this group is excluded from the civil dialogue and, to a large extent, the exercise of active citizenship. EYF (2010a) is particularly critical of EU youth policy (Youth in Action):

> Young people with fewer opportunities and small youth organizations do not have the capacity to build the knowledge necessary to benefit from the Youth in Action programme and from most of the EU programmes (...). The European civil society should be strengthened by including a truly European level within the programme and a recognition of the status of European youth organizations who are the main channels through which young people interact structurally with the EU democratic process (p. 5).

EYF's criticism concentrates on mechanisms for engagement. It highlights the crucial role played by OCS in facilitating access to institutional structures. EYF's work on strengthening transnational cooperation provides evidence of a process of Europeanization, whilst also highlighting the linchpin role played by OCS in mediating between the national and the European level. We explore this in more detail in Bee and Guerrina (2014) where we look at how social problems—e.g. poverty, racism, unemployment, discrimination, and social exclusion—negatively affect the ability of weaker groups to participate and engage in the process of Europeanization.

Political Participation and Civil Dialogue

Brussels-based organizations have long recognized the importance of developing some form of civil dialogue[3] and have sought to promote active citizenship as a policy rather than just a set of practices involving interactions between citizens, national and transnational organizations, and European institutions. In practice, however, national NGOs struggle to establish coherent patterns of representation, which ultimately limits their influence at the EU level. It is worth noting that European-level civil society organizations have been elaborating specific dialogic instruments to facilitate interest representation at the supranational level.

Our analysis of civil society statements and policy documents highlights the centrality of civil dialogue. This process has an enabling function in as far as it facilitates access to actors within the EU institutions and allows direct input in agenda-setting mechanisms. It guarantees transparent interplay between EU institutional actors and NGOs and enables the exercise of active citizenship. As Social Platform (2010) recently stated: 'Civil dialogue is a concrete tool to strengthen the relationship between public decision makers and CSOs'. This is thus a formal instrument through which NGOs lobby, frame claims, and establish a dialogic relationship with the policy-makers. It is therefore meant to establish a bidirectional model of institutional communication at the European level.

Recognition of civil dialogue as a core practice for European governance came with the inclusion of Art. 11 in the Lisbon Treaty, whereby

> The institutions shall maintain an open, transparent and regular dialogue with representative associations and civil society. (Art. 11.2)

> The European Commission shall carry out broad consultations with parties concerned in order to ensure that the Union's actions are coherent and transparent. (Art. 11.3)

Both these practices have long been a feature of EU policy-making. However, inclusion in the Treaty provides a legal foundation; it reiterates the centrality of interest representation and fosters active citizenship as a core practice for the delivery of democratic governance at the European level. The ENAR (2009) welcomes this shift:

> It is not only representative democracy which will be strengthened by the text of the Lisbon Treaty. The explicit adoption of the principle of participatory democracy is an extremely important innovation in the Lisbon Treaty from the perspective of advocacy groups working in the field of racism and xenophobia. (p. 13)

Article 11 therefore provides a much needed opening for OCS to become formally involved in policy-making processes. This is an important shift that paves the way for a wide range of interests and voices to find the way to the negotiating table. It also raises important questions about the very nature of European-level OCS and interests represented within it. Increasing institutionalization of OCS is a clear opportunity to shape the policy agenda; however, it also carries the inherent danger that OCS will lose its critical voice.

It is important to recognize the potential of active citizenship and civic engagement; however, both practices should not be seen as being fully inclusive. For instance, in our sample, the OCS points at a number of issues that undermine the effectiveness of civil dialogue. A recurrent meta-narrative on this account points at the limited reach of Art. 11 in relation to weaker groups. Civil society's demands for more structured forms of dialogue and for the development of a symmetrical system of institutional communication have yet to be completely fulfilled. What is clear from this brief discussion is that OCS does not deem Art. 11 to be sufficient to bridge the participation gap affecting European governance.

In a 2010 report, the ENAR discussed '15 principles for framing a positive approach to migration'. Lack of inclusion and silencing of minority groups are key concerns of the organization:

> The current process has been marked by a lack of dialogue and engagement with civil society. It is crucial that such a dialogue takes place as it is central to the development of a common European policy on immigration and asylum (...) In order to change the negative dynamic around the migration debate, the migrants' voice must be heard in EU and national decision making concerning migration policy. (ENAR, 2010, pp. 5, 11)

In a similar vein, an EYF (2010b) policy paper looking at the issue of *Young People and Poverty* highlights the condition of disadvantaged groups and at the possible policy responses in order to improve their social inclusion:

> Unfortunately, it needs to be said that poverty and social exclusion affect active citizenship, hinder participation and set barriers for volunteering. Youth organisations, in their daily activities often, contribute to the activation and empowerment of young disadvantaged people that can eventually allow them to break away from the vicious circle of poverty. (p. 10)

These extracts highlight two issues that are important for the analysis presented here: first, OCS is uniquely positioned to provide a platform for interest representation and inclusion. They are the critical voice of European policy-making. They serve a key function in articulating counter-discourses and narratives, thus providing checks and balances for institutional agendas. Second, the inclusion of OCS into formal processes allows greater influence on policy-making at the agenda-setting stages; however, it also dilutes its ability to exercise its role as a critical voice.

European Social Dimension

What emerges from the analysis of the previous nodal points is that civil society organizations identified the need to develop a European social dimension as a top policy priority for the future. This umbrella concept allows for contestation of key values underpinning the process as a whole. It therefore becomes the *discursive battleground* identified by Diez (2001).

Social policy forces public institutions to address questions that are normative in nature and outcomes. Issues like sustainability, gender equality, health promotion, and anti-discrimination require detailed consideration of the foundational values of the organizations, how key actors adopt and promote these values, and the limitations of specific strategies. Focus on the social dimension therefore provides an opening for OCS to raise questions about the applicability of the key institutional narratives and delivery mechanism, e.g. the Lisbon Strategy. This process of exchange, challenge, and reframing allows both public institutions and civil society to refine their position, aims, and role within the European policy-making process.

It is important to note that a number of Brussels-based organizations advocate for the development of a European social dimension based on the principle of equality. The principle has been included in the founding treaties and has been altered in subsequent iterations by preserving its centrality. In addition, a large body of secondary legislation and public statements place equality at the heart of the integration process. Despite these, our analytical sample produced a number of significant criticisms of the approach adopted by the Commission in its implementation. For example, commenting on the Barroso II presidency, the EWL (2010):

> Equality between women and men is a fundamental right and value of the European Union and should be central to all Commission initiatives, policies and programmes. It is a legal, moral and economic imperative, not a luxury to be addressed sporadically or only during times of prosperity. While some positive steps are being prepared in this area—including a new Commission action plan on equality between women and men which will hopefully give flesh and bones to commitments—so far, the Barroso II Commission's performance has been disturbingly mixed, and concrete actions in favour of a more equal society have been few.

The EWL's position provides a test for the Commission's rhetoric/narrative, particularly when the dominant perception is that it has not been accompanied by substantive action. It also highlights some of the limitations of a social agenda that is deeply normative in nature but is operating in a political context where the polity is largely absent and policy-makers are seen as setting the agenda for social change.

Of particular concern to organizations like the EWL, the ENAR, and the Social Platform is the issue of intersectionality. Mainstreaming the specific social needs and social problems affecting different minorities into European policies thus becomes a top priority. The EWL's (2009) contribution to the consultation on the roadmap for gender equality and the follow-up strategy makes this position very clear:

> One of the related challenges has been that the gender angle is often forgotten in policy areas that are not seen as related to gender equality, e.g. disability, Roma inclusion or integration, migration and asylum, while in turn this other policy angle is overlooked in gender equality policies. This shows the need to increase policy coherence and effectively monitor gender mainstreaming in other policy areas while there is also a need to strengthen the intersectional approach in the new Strategic Action Plan (...). Without the effective implementation of an intersectional approach, the specific needs of some groups of women (...) might be overlooked in the policy areas covered by the Strategic Action Plan. (p. 4)

This extract highlights increasing concern with the approach of European institutions that seem to adopt a very one-dimensional view of equality. With preferential access to the Commission the EWL therefore provides a very useful source of—constructive—critique for European political institutions. What is significant here is that these shortcomings remain central to gender governance despite the fact that equality between men and women is also one of the most developed areas of European social policy (Guerrina, 2005) and the EWL has a long-standing relationship with the European Commission and the European Parliament.

Remaining on the issue of anti-discrimination, the ENAR (2009) states its position in relation to the challenges that different minority communities have faced in gaining support and recognition at the European level:

> The only area of anti-racist work which has received specific high level political attention has been the particularly hostile social and economic conditions in which the Roma, especially in the new member states of central and Eastern Europe, find themselves. Consequently, the incorporation of equality mainstreaming, including the mainstreaming of anti-racism, in the Lisbon Treaty, represents a significant strengthening of the existing legal basis for current practices and for policy-making. (p. 12)

In this context ENAR's work focuses on identifying the limitations of current policy discourse. Similar to the previous example, the role of this civil society organization is to act as a 'critical friend', working closely with institutional bodies to improve policy outcomes. There is little evidence, however, of how these criticisms have been folded into the actual policy process. ENAR and EWL also have preferential access to European institutions, which on the one hand provides a platform to influence directly the policy process but on the other positions them as the dominant voice of each group at the European level.

Some policy priorities surface that require urgent attention: enhancing intercultural dialogue and the establishment of common anti-discrimination frameworks across EU and non-EU states; recognition of disadvantaged groups—e.g. ethnic and linguistic minorities, women and youth from minority groups—by guaranteeing access to education and the labour market; development of policy frameworks in the areas of healthy living and sustainability; and the establishment of concrete measures regarding social Europe.

Given the shortcomings of the EPS, the most effective way to communicate with the polity is within a national framework. Key information campaigns and education programmes need to be established by national institutions to facilitate public communications on issues like gender equality, rights of minorities, possibilities to access the labour market, etc. The recent Euro crisis and associated debates about the reach and depth of austerity are poignant examples of the importance of public communication and the dominance of national public spaces. Key drivers of social Europe, such as social solidarity and social cohesion, are questioned and reframed in this context.

In thinking about the process of polity building in which the EU is currently engaged, the development of a European social dimension is central to the long-term success of the project. Yet policies coming under this broad umbrella still lack visibility. One obvious conclusion is that political institutions must improve public communication measures at the national level. This is, however, unlikely as official communication will inevitably fall between European and national interests. Improving the engagement and access of national NGOs in the supranational setting is likely to be a more effective strategy. Civil society organizations thus become the vehicle for public communication.

Conclusion

This article has looked at the role of civil society organizations in European governance. Our analysis highlights that OCS is not only a central actor in the EPS, but also plays a fundamental role in respect to European democratization and constitutionalism. The diverse set of interests it represents, or attempts to represent, widens the bases for political participation and representation at the European level. OCS plays a key role in shifting and readdressing the EU's policy-making on questions of public interest and for developing transnational forms of social solidarity.

The development of a networked EU and the growth in the role and importance of non-state actors is strategically oriented towards the debate on the EPS. As explained in this article, this is constituted by a constellation of actors that elaborate diverging and conflicting discourses at different levels. In the European Discursive Battleground (Diez, 2001), different publics struggle to shape meanings on the social reality, to influence the policy-making and to frame the public policies. The final section of this article highlights the asymmetrical nature of OCS. Brussels-based organizations are an expression of a strong public, representing transnational actors and attempting to include the subnational and weak publics. The EPS that emerges in this process favours interest representation through strong civil society organizations. The downside of this approach is that the organizations become socialized and institutionalized through the exchange. The capacity of these organizations to formulate a counter-discourse, thus expanding the reach of democratic governance in Europe, is therefore diminished.

It has been argued that the emergence of the EPS is contextual to the emergence of a debate about the feasibility of a model of institutional communication. This ambitious project was a reaction to the rejection of the Constitutional Treaty in 2005 and of the Lisbon Treaty in 2008. It is based on the assumption that the democratic deficit arises from a communication deficit. This reflects the process that followed the draft of the White Paper on Governance in 2001, when the European Commission declared that 'the aim should be to create a transnational "space" where citizens from different countries can discuss what they perceive as being the important challenges for the Union' (CEC, 2001, p. 12). At that time, Eriksen (2001, p. 2) commented,

> [B]y focusing on apathy and ignorance, one not only puts the blame on the people, but also reduces the problem to one of information—it is about lack of knowledge. This represents a rather superficial understanding of the causes of the distrust, and one which, nevertheless, remains at odds with the post-Nice-debate.

Popular rejection of the Constitutional Treaty in 2005 supports Eriksen's criticism of the Commission's approach. However, this time the Commission's efforts to foster active citizenship must be acknowledged; they resulted in the drafting of public policies in areas like health, gender equality, environment, global warming, and anti-discrimination.

This public policy approach is based on 'a citizen-centred strategy'. This is supported by the development of a Europe-wide, homogenous public sphere. Unfortunately, this approach suffers from a mis-conceptualization of the EPS and a tendency to favour national models. The strategy of the European Commission has not taken into account some of the main findings of current research on the EPS, e.g. the existence of fragmented and overlapping discourses, the fluidity of the processes of transnationalization, and the existence of different power structures that define access to policy-making and thus influence on the policy agenda. Ultimately, it disregards the diversity in European publics. The present scenario is characterized by the presence of a whole set of counter-discourses going on in Brussels and entailing a continuous discursive confrontation between different publics in the struggle to fix a meaning on the practices of active citizenship.

Notes

1. MAGEEQ: Multiple Meanings of Gender Equality. See http://www.mageeq.net/.
2. The documents were selected through the use of a series of key words to search in each organization's database. The initial sample included 45 documents (15 per category of citizen). On the basis of their relevance for our research question, we then selected 18 documents (6 per category). The analysis was executed with the support of a protocol for the analysis of policy documents divided into seven core sub-categories: policy actors, policy context, policy priorities, policy debates, EU policies, European crisis, and counter-discourse.
3. Civil dialogue is not to be confused with social dialogue. In its 2006 report *Civil Dialogue: Making It Work Better*, the Civil Society Contact Group draws the difference between the two and argues that civil dialogue is 'developed as a parallel to that of social dialogue, it refers to a wide range of interactions between civil society organisations and institutions rather than a clear-cut set of practices' (CSCG, 2006, p. 22).

References

Balme, R. & Chabanet, D (2008) *European Governance and Democracy: Power and Protest in the EU* (Lanham: Rowman & Littlefield).

Bee, C. (2010) Understanding the EU's institutional communication. Principles and structure of a contested policy, in: C. Bee & E. Bozzini (Eds) *Mapping the European Public Sphere: Institutions, Media and Civil Society*, pp. 83–98 (Aldershot: Ashgate Publishing).

Bee, C. & Guerrina, R. (2014) The Europeanisation of policy discourses on participation and active citizenship, in: M. Barrett & B. Zani (Eds) *Political and Civic Engagement: Multidisciplinary Perspectives* (London: Routledge) (in press).

Bellamy, R. (2010) Democracy without democracy? Can the EU's democratic 'outputs' be separated from the democratic 'inputs' provided by competitive parties and majority rule? *Journal of European Public Policy*, 17(1), pp. 2–19.

Bellamy, R. & Castiglione, D. (2000) The uses of democracy: Reflections on the European democratic deficit, in: J. E. Eriksen & E. O. Fossum (Eds) *Democracy in the EU: Integration Through Deliberation*, pp. 65–84 (London: Routledge).

Bozzini, E. (2007) The role of civil society organisations in written consultation processes: From the European Monitoring Centre to the European Fundamental Rights Agency, in: V. Della Sala & C. Ruzza (Eds) *Governance and Civil Society: Policy Perspectives*, pp. 93–109 (Manchester: Manchester University Press).

Calhoun, C. (2002) Imagining solidarity: Cosmopolitanism, constitutional patriotism, and the public sphere, *Public Culture*, 14(1), pp. 147–171.

Calhoun, C. (2003) The democratic integration of Europe: Interests, identity, and the public sphere, in: M. Berezin & M. Schain (Eds) *Europe Without Borders. Remapping Territory*, pp. 243–274 (Baltimore and London: The Johns Hopkins University Press).

Castells, M. (1996) *The Rise of the Network Society* (Cambridge: Blackwell).

CEC (2001) *European Governance: A White Paper*, COM (2001) 428 final. (Brussels: European Commission).

CEC (2005) *The Commission's Contribution to the Period of Reflection and Beyond: Plan-D for Democracy, Dialogue and Debate*, COM (2005) 494 final. (Brussels: European Commission).

CEC (2006) *White Paper on a European Communication Policy*, COM (2006) 35 final. (Brussels: European Commission).

Christiansen, T., Jorgensen, K. E. & Wiener, A. (1999) The social construction of Europe, *Journal of European Public Policy*, 6(4), pp. 528–544.

Coen, D. (2007) Empirical and theoretical studies in EU lobbying, *Journal of European Public Policy*, 14(3), pp. 333–345.

CSCG (2006) Civil dialogue: Making it work better. Available at http://www.stakeholders-socialinclusion.eu/site/en/tools/2006-1 (accessed 1 September 2013).

Della Porta, D. (Ed.) (2009) *Another Europe* (London: Routledge).

Diez, T. (2001) Europe as a discursive battleground: Discourse analysis and European integration studies, *Cooperation and Conflict*, 36(1), pp. 5–38.

Díez-Medrano, J. (2003) *Framing Europe. Attitudes to European Integration in Germany, Spain, and the United Kingdom* (Princeton, NJ: Princeton University Press).

Dryzek, J. S. (2008) Policy analysis as critique, in: M. Moran, M. Rein & R. E. Goodin (Eds) *The Oxford Handbook of Public Policy*, pp. 190–203 (Oxford: Oxford University Press).

ENAR (2008) 15 principles for framing a positive approach to migration. Available at http://cms.horus.be/files/99935/MediaArchive/pdf/MigrationPublication_EN_Lowres.pdf (accessed 30 March 2013).

ENAR (2009) The EU Lisbon Treaty: What implications for anti-racism? Available at http://cms.horus.be/files/99935/MediaArchive/publications/lisbontreaty_EN_LRfinal.pdf (accessed 30 March 2013).

ENAR (2010) *Combating Racist Crime and Violence: Testimonies and Advocacy Strategies*. Available at http://cms.horus.be/files/99935/MediaArchive/pdf/AdvocacyBooklet_EN_lowres.pdf (accessed 30 March 2013).

Eriksen, E. O. (2001) Democratic or technocratic governance? *Jean Monnet Working Paper. Symposium: Mountain or Molehill? A Critical Appraisal of the Commission White Paper on Governance 06/01*. Available at http://www.eui.eu/Documents/RSCAS/Research/OnlineSymposia/Amstrong.pdf (accessed 23 October 2013).

Eriksen, E. O. (2004) Conceptualizing European public spheres: General, segmented and strong publics, *ARENA Working Paper 3/04*. Available at http://www.sv.uio.no/arena/english/research/projects/cidel/old/WorkshopStirling/PaperEriksen.pdf (accessed 23 October 2013).

Eriksen, E. O. & Fossum, J. E. (Eds) (2000) *Democracy in the European Union: Integration Through Deliberation* (London: Routledge).

Eriksen, E. O. & Fossum, J. E. (2002) Democracy through strong publics in the European Union? *Journal of Common Market Studies*, 40(3), pp. 401–424.

EurActiv (2006) *Yellow Paper on European Communication. EurActiv's Plan D: Diversify, Decentralise, Disseminate, Decide*. Available at http://www.euractiv.com/29/images/YellowPaperFinal30September2006_tcm29-159859.pdf (accessed 30 March 2013).

EWL (2009) EWL response to the consultation on the roadmap for equality between women and men 2006–2010 and follow-up strategy. Available at http://www.womenlobby.org/spip.php?article398 (accessed 30 March 2013).

EWL (2010) Barroso II and women's rights. Available at http://www.womenlobby.org/spip.php?article451 (accessed 30 March 2013).

EYF (2010a) *Position Paper on Youth in Action 2.0*. Available at http://youth-partnership-eu.coe.int/youth-partnership/documents/EKCYP/Youth_Policy/docs/YP_strategies/Policy/YIA2-0_FINAL.pdf (accessed 30 March 2013).

EYF (2010b) *Policy Paper On Young People and Poverty*. Available at http://youth-partnership-eu.coe.int/youth-partnership/documents/EKCYP/Youth_Policy/docs/Cohesion/Policy/Young_People_Poverty_FINAL.pdf (accessed 30 March 2013).

Fawkes, J. (2004) Public relations and communications, in: A. Theaker (Ed.) *The Public Relations Handbook*, pp. 18–31 (London: Routledge).

Fraser, N. (1992) Rethinking the public sphere: A contribution to the critique of actually existing democracy, in: C. Calhoun (Ed.) *Habermas and the Public Sphere*, pp. 109–142 (Cambridge, MA: MIT Press).

Fraser, N. (1995) Politics culture and the public sphere: Toward a postmodern conception, in: L. Nicholson & S. Seidman (Eds) *Social Postmodernism Beyond Identity Politics*, pp. 287–312 (Cambridge: Cambridge University Press).

Greenwood, J. (2007) *Interest Representation in the European Union* (Basingstoke: Palgrave Macmillan).

Grimm, D. (1995) Does Europe need a constitution? *European Law Journal*, 1(3), pp. 282–302.

Grunig, A. & Grunig, J. E. (1992) Models of public relations and communication, in: J. E. Grunig (Ed.) *Excellence in Public Relations and Communication Management*, pp. 285–326 (Hillsdale, NJ: Lawrence Erlbaum Associates).

Guerrina, R. (2002) *Europe: History, Ideas and Ideologies* (London: Arnold).

Guerrina, R. (2005) *Mothering the Union The Politics of Gender, Equality and Maternity Rights in the EU* (Manchester: Manchester University Press).

Habermas, J. (1989) *The Structural Transformation of the Public Sphere: An Inquiry into a Category of Bourgeois Society* (Cambridge: Polity Press).

Habermas, J. (1995) Comment on the paper by Dieter Grimm 'Does Europe need a constitution?', *European Law Journal*, 1(3), pp. 303–307.

Hajer, M. (2002) Discourse analysis and the study of policy making, *European Political Science*, 2(1), pp. 61–65.

Hajer, M. A. & Wagenaar, H. (Eds) (2003) *Deliberative Policy Analysis: Understanding Governance in the Network Society* (Cambridge: Cambridge University Press).

Harrison, J. & Wessels, B. (Eds) (2009) *Mediating Europe. Mass Media, Mass Communication and the European Public Sphere* (Oxford: Berghahn).

Howart, D. & Torfing, J. (2005) *Discourse Theory in European Politics* (Basingstoke: Palgrave Macmillan).

Ingram, H. & Schneider, A. L. (2008) Policy analysis for democracy, in: M. Moran, M. Rein & R. E. Goodin (Eds) *The Oxford Handbook of Public Policy*, pp. 169–189 (Oxford: Oxford University Press).

Kingdon, J. W. (2011) *Agendas, Alternatives and Public Policies* (Crawfordsville: Longman).

Kohler-Koch, B. & Rittberger, B. (Eds) (2007) *Debating the Democratic Legitimacy of the European Union* (Lanham: Rowman & Littlefield).

Koopmans, R. & Pfetsch, B. (2003) Towards a Europeanised public sphere? Comparing political actors and the media in Germany, *ARENA Working Paper 23*. Available at http://www.sv.uio.no/arena/english/research/publications/arena-publications/workingpapers/working-papers2003/wp03_23.pdf (last accessed 23 October 2013).

Laclau, E. & Mouffe, C. (1985) *Hegemony and Socialist Strategy: Towards a Radical Democratic Politics* (London: Verso).

Liebert, U. (2007) Introduction: Structuring political conflict about Europe: National media in transnational discourse analysis, *Perspectives on European Politics and Society*, 8(3), pp. 235–260.

Mancini, P. (2003) *Manuale di comunicazione pubblica* (Roma and Bari: Laterza).

Ruzza, C. (2004) *Europe and Civil Society: Movements Coalitions and European Governance* (Manchester: Manchester University Press).

Ruzza, C. & Bozzini, E. (2008) Organised civil society and European governance: Routes of contestation, *European Political Science*, 7(3), pp. 296–303.

Sánchez-Salgado, R. (2007) Giving a European dimension to civil society organizations, *Journal of Civil Society*, 3(3), pp. 253–269.

Sassatelli, M. (2009) *Becoming Europeans: Cultural Identity and Cultural Policies* (Basingstoke: Palgrave Macmillan).

Scharpf, F. (1998) Demokratie in der transnationalen Politik, in: U. Beck (Ed.) *Politik in der Globaliserung*, pp. 228–253 (Frankfurt a. M.: Suhrkamp).

Schlesinger, P. (1999) Changing spaces of political communication: The case of the European Union, *Political Communication*, 16(3), pp. 263–279.

Schlesinger, P. (2003) The Babel of Europe. An essay on networks and communicative spaces, *ARENA Working Paper 22*. Available at http://www.sv.uio.no/arena/english/research/publications/arena-publications/workingpapers/working-papers2003/wp03_22.pdf (last accessed 23 October 2013).

Schlesinger, P. & Kevin, D. (2000) Can the European Union become a sphere of publics? in: E. O. Eriksen & J. E. Fossum (Eds) *Democracy in the European Union: Integration Through Deliberation?* pp. 206–229 (London: Routledge).

Schulz-Forberg, H. (2010) Cosmopolitanism or ethnic homogeneity? Roma identity, European integration and the European public sphere, in: C. Bee & E. Bozzini (Eds) *Mapping the European Public Sphere: Institutions, Media and Civil Society*, pp. 177–194 (Aldershot: Ashgate Publishing).

Shore, C. (2000) *Building Europe: The Cultural Politics of European Integration* (London: Routledge).

Smismans, S. (Ed.) (2006) *Civil Society and Legitimate European Governance* (Cheltenham: Edward Elgar).

Social Platform (2008) *Annual Conference 2008 Report for Workshop 4: New Faces in Europe: How Can We Connect with the 'Hard to Reach' Communities Across the EU?* Available at http://cms.horus.be/files/99907/MediaArchive/Events/Annual_conferences/SPAC_Workshop4_hard.pdf (accessed 30 March 2013).

Social Platform (2010) How to establish an effective dialogue between the EU and civil society organisations. Available at http://cms.horus.be/files/99907/MediaArchive/Policies/Participatory_democracy/SocialPlatform_EffectiveCivilDialogue.pdf (accessed 30 March 2013).

Statham, P. (2007) Political communication, European integration and the transformation of national public spheres: A comparison of Britain and France, in: J. E. Fossum & P. Schlesinger (Eds) *The European Union and the Public Sphere: A Communicative Space in the Making?*, pp. 110–134 (London: Routledge).

Trenz, H. J. (2010) The Europeanisation of political communication: Conceptual clarifications and empirical measurement, in: C. Bee & E. Bozzini (Eds) *Mapping the European Public Sphere: Institutions, Media and Civil Society*, pp. 15–30 (Aldershot: Ashgate Publishing).

Trenz, H. J. & Eder, K. (2004) The democratising role of a European public sphere. Towards a model of democratic functionalism, *Journal of European Social Theory*, 7(1), pp. 5–25.

Van de Steeg, M. (2002) Rethinking the conditions for a public sphere in the European Union, *European Journal of Social Theory*, 5(4), pp. 499–519.

Verloo, M. (2005) Mainstreaming gender equality in Europe. A critical frame analysis approach, *The Greek Review of Social Research*, 117(B), pp. 11–34.

Warleigh, A. (2001) Europeanizing civil society: NGOs as agents of political socialization in the European Union, *Journal of Common Market Studies*, 39(4), pp. 619–639.

Europe as a Beacon of Democracy? Citizenship Policies Relating to Youth and Migrants in Portugal

NORBERTO RIBEIRO, CARLA MALAFAIA,
MARIA FERNANDES-JESUS, TIAGO NEVES & ISABEL MENEZES

Faculdade de Psicologia e de Ciências da Educação, Centro de Investigação e Intervenção Educativas (CIIE), Universidade do Porto, Porto, Portugal

ABSTRACT *This article aims to compare discourses about national and European policies on active citizenship and democratic participation, with a particular focus on youth and migrants. For this purpose we analysed official documents of public institutions and nongovernmental organizations (NGOs) in order to assess how the process of Europeanization has influenced national policies with regard to increasing political participation and citizens' civic awareness. Additionally, we conducted interviews with policy makers and NGO leaders in order to integrate and compare different levels of discourse and thus identify potential dissonances. Analysis of the documents shows that there is a strong concern to match national policy priorities with those established by international organizations. Notwithstanding positive perceptions, NGO leaders and policy makers criticize the ways policies have been implemented, stressing the need to adopt a strategy that bridges the gap between the prescribed and the real, as well as the importance of overcoming the hegemony of economic factors in policy decisions. In this regard, NGO leaders criticize the cynicism of political leaders and policies motivated by demographic and economic concerns. In relation to European identity and integration, NGO leaders argue that Europe must be collectively constructed; yet, policy makers stress that the failure of the Constitutional Treaty in 2005 resulted from a deficit in the negotiation process. In sum, this article suggests that it is necessary to promote greater involvement of civil society in the design and implementation of policies which, in turn, may contribute to the strengthening of shared democratic principles.*

Introduction

The European Union is currently facing one of the most significant challenges to its political evolution since the ratification of the founding treaties. On the one hand, it was awarded the Nobel Peace Prize in 2012 for its commitment to stability and peace in

Europe; on the other hand, the last couple of years have been marked by intense social and economic unrest. The growth of demonstrations such as 'Geração à Rasca' in Portugal, 'Indignados' in Spain, or 'Occupy Brussels', mainly contesting high rates of unemployment among young people and opposition to European austerity, are a clear example of increasing social conflict and an expression of lack of trust in political institutions, culminating in a challenge to the legitimacy of European governance and institutions.

Several international studies show that low levels of civic and political participation are more apparent in young people (Benedicto & Morán, 2002; Perliger et al., 2006). Research developed in the Portuguese context has been only partially in line with this analysis (Ferreira, 2006; Veiga, 2008; Azevedo, 2009). Indeed, although Portuguese young people do have low levels of civic and political participation, they are nonetheless more involved in civic and political issues than adults (Magalhães & Moral, 2008). Significantly, some literature points to a 'participatory revolution' (Norris, 2002) or, as more recently stated by Menezes et al. (2012), a 'paradoxical movement'. That is, against the common notion of a detached youth, some authors have been arguing that new forms of participation are emerging, with young people involved in meaningful experiences (Norris, 2002; Juris & Pleyers, 2009). This means that we are witnessing a generational change, with young people investing in forms of civic and political participation beyond conventional ones (cf. Putnam, 2000; Zukin et al., 2006; Marsh et al., 2007). This literature suggests that it is not so much a lack of commitment on the part of young people, but rather them finding new ways of exercising their citizenship (Harris et al., 2010) based in less institutionalized political practices and in more horizontal forms of participation (Norris, 2002; Menezes et al., 2012).

However, even if it is true that the ways young people participate are changing, it is equally true that they value traditional forms of political participation less, which may lead to youth becoming detached from the higher, formal instances in which collective decisions that affect our societies are taken.

Research also stresses that immigrants are another disadvantaged group when it comes to civic and political participation (cf. Ahmad & Pinnock, 2007; Lopez & Marcelo, 2008), particularly in terms of their limited access to political rights (e.g. the right to vote and to stand as candidates in local elections). In this context, youth and migrants are two groups that tend to be on the margins of the political processes and, therefore, at increased risk of exclusion. For this reason, this article takes both these groups as the main units of analysis.

The analysis presented here fits into the debate about post-national citizenship (cf. Benhabib, 1999; Janoski, 2000; Carvalhais, 2004) which calls for a more inclusive understanding of citizenship. Carvalhais (2004, p. 17) argues that all members of the polity 'are equally instructed of democratic participation rights and of full communication, enabling them in equality and freedom to be active parts in the decision processes that potentially affect them'—an empowering project that implies that nation states are willing to debate the criteria underlying citizenship rights.

However, the application of those principles in the European Union (EU) has been disappointing, particularly if we consider the implementation of very restrictive policies, such as the 'Return Directive'[1] which establishes common standards and procedures in Member States for returning illegal migrants. Therefore, these policies strengthen the idea, already denounced by Benhabib, that 'a two-tiered status of foreignness is developing throughout Europe. There are different rights and privileges accorded to each category of foreigner within member states' (1999, p. 716). Recent developments in EU social politics highlight the need to re-engage with these debates. Increasingly restrictive immigration policies and high levels of youth unemployment are crystallizing social hierarchies and exclusions from—at least the more formal and traditional—political processes.

Several studies show that immigration policies play an important role in shaping the civic and political participation of immigrants, i.e. their effective integration[2] in the host country (cf. Ireland, 1994; Soysal, 1994; Geddes, 2000; Koopmans & Statham, 2000; Koopmans, 2004; Hooghe, 2005; Schrover & Vermeulen, 2005). For instance, Koopmans (2004), in his comparative analysis of the involvement of migrants and ethnic minorities in public debates and mobilization in Germany, the Netherlands, and the UK, considers that local and national integration and citizenship regimes can be seen as political opportunity structures that may stimulate, inhibit, or prevent immigrants' involvement and participation. In Portugal, existing research has reached similar conclusions regarding the influence of institutional and political opportunities on the participation of immigrants (Teixeira & Albuquerque, 2005; Sardinha, 2007). Sardinha (2007) stresses that, despite the funding provided for immigrants' associations by the Portuguese State, the existing policies are not effective. Immigrants' civic and political participation is limited by their social status.

Low levels of political participation among foreign-born immigrants have also been explored. Zobel and Barbosa (2009), for example, stress the need to consider the influence of several elements of the Portuguese political context in order to effectively improve immigrants' political integration. In that sense, they criticize, first, the poor use (that is made) of laws that guarantee the rights of active and passive political participation. They believe this is caused by the frailties of a state that does not complement political and legal innovation with assessment and information strategies. Second, the stress on the importance of the principle of reciprocity in the debate around the 1996 Act[3] (that, broadly speaking, allows foreigners the political right to vote and be elected on the condition that the same rights are granted to the Portuguese citizens abroad) indicates that Portugal still holds interest in excluding a significant proportion of immigrants. Finally, the fact that political parties have not exhibited any clear position on the issue of immigrant voting or on the possibilities of their integration into their structures indicates that the political rights of immigrants are still not a priority when compared to their economic and social rights—as Carvalhais (2006, pp. 58–59) concludes, Portugal's recognition of post-national citizenship is tenuous.

In a different yet related vein, other studies report that some groups of immigrants distrust the state (cf. Marques & Santos, 2004; Grassi, 2007, 2009; Menezes et al., 2012). Grassi (2007), for instance, shows that young Angolans mainly distrust strangers (51%), but also local government politicians (42%) and central government politicians (39%), although national studies also show that young Portuguese distrust the political institutions as well (Menezes et al., 2005), and feel sceptical regarding the effectiveness of traditional politics (Magalhães & Moral, 2008). In another study, Grassi (2009) also points out that young Cape Verdeans do not trust the Portuguese Government and more than half of them feel that little or no attention is given to immigrants by the Portuguese executive.

In sum, as the criticisms pointed out by the literature suggest, the current socio-political context might be interpreted as presenting a dissatisfaction of young people and immigrants with national and European policies that resonates with Benhabib's criticism: 'Europe has ceased to be an ideal, for some it has long become an illusion' (1999, p. 714).

Research Questions, Methodology, and Data

This article aims to compare institutional and civil society discourses about European and Portuguese national policies on active citizenship and democratic participation,[4] with a particular focus on young people and migrants. To do so, we analysed official documents of public institutions (PIs) and nongovernmental organizations (NGOs) in order to explore how the process of Europeanization has influenced national policies that aim to foster citizens' political participation and civic awareness, particularly at the European level. Document analysis focused on discourses on key political issues (e.g. European citizenship, European social policies, and the European public sphere). More specifically, we examined the visibility of European issues; the alignment of national policies with European standards; criticism of European policies; and the development of the 'European dimension'.

Our analysis recognizes the existence of significant discrepancies between policy makers, official documents, and implementation mechanisms. In order to highlight these competing narratives and objectives, we carried out interviews with NGO leaders and policy makers. These interviews allowed us to integrate and contrast different levels of discourse and thus identify potential dissonances. Like the analysis of documents, the interviews aimed to map the convergence of European priorities and national priorities; define patterns of Europeanization in the context of national policies; identify the visibility of European policies at the national level; and evaluate the impact of European legislation and policy making at the national level. To this end, the interviews were structured around three key dimensions: political priorities and institutional views on those priorities; European priorities; and European integration, to account for the personal opinion of participants regarding, for example, the Constitutional Treaty of 2005, the Lisbon Treaty, and the existence of a democratic deficit in the EU.

The study adopted a qualitative approach that enabled the exploration of narratives and political objectives through the application of discourse analysis to selected documents and interviews. The main assumption underlying this theoretical–methodological approach was that language reflects the structures and dynamics of power within society in general and politics in particular (cf. Hajer, 2002; Hajer, 2005; Howarth & Torfing, 2005). Thus, this approach was used in the analysis of the dominant discourses in the documents and interviews in order to enable the identification of policy priorities and their impact on policy outcomes. In other words, this approach, as argued by Hajer (2005, p. 300),

> would illuminate a particular *discursive structure* in the discussion of the policy towards, say, immigration in the European Union. Here a discourse analysis would bring out a certain regularity in the particular ideas, concepts, and categories *in which terms* immigration is discussed. In addition, it identifies the practices in which this discourse gets reproduced. (emphasis in the original)

To be sure, we acknowledge that this theoretical–methodological approach may raise discussion about the level of analytical detail needed. Being aware of this, we follow Hajer (2005, p. 308) and focus on 'emblematic issues' to overcome the 'false dichotomy of detail versus relevance'.

The study looked at 22 documents: 12 from NGOs, six for each area (youth and migrants), and 10 documents from PIs, resulting from the selection of five documents for each area. Eight interviews were conducted and analysed: five NGO leaders who have worked in the fields of youth and migrants, and three policy makers working at the national level in the two areas. The choice of NGO leaders and policy makers was influenced by the relevance of their work in the two fields considered.

Document Analysis: Main Findings

This section sets out key trends in the development of a policy framework and the interactions between civil society organizations, national institutional structure, and European policies. This helps us establish how youth, migrants, and related policies are positioned within the wider policy framework. It also highlights continuities and dis-junctures in the way policies are formulated and implemented. European policy trends are discussed in the light of the dominant discourses presented in official documents of PIs and NGOs. In a political context that has been characterized by the 'crisis of Europe', brought to the fore by the failure of the Constitutional Treaty in 2005 and by Ireland's rejection of the Lisbon Treaty in 2008, particular attention is paid to the European dimension and to the criticisms of the European project in both PI and NGO documents.

Youth

One of the main concerns in the youth-related documents analysed relates to the decline in civic and political participation among young people and how to find strategies to stimulate and improve the way they engage in society. The main issues raised are: (1) the level and quality of participation in a society that is undergoing profound transformation; (2) how youth can be an active part of this change; and (3) how to overcome the difficulties and anxieties that young people feel about their responsibility for social renewal. Areas such as employment, housing, education, and training are considered factors that influence participation opportunities. These concerns, in fact, match the overall objectives of the EU Youth Strategy, which seeks 'to provide more and equal opportunities for young people in education and in the labour market' and 'to encourage young people to be active citizens and participate in society'.[5] The values most often mentioned in relation to youth policies are civic participation, respect for diversity, human rights, democracy, and sustainable development. In addition, it is considered necessary to strengthen youth organizations at the municipal level.

In general, Portuguese PIs have adopted the following goals to increase the participation of young people: (1) promote the creation and development of partnerships that enable the improvement of interventions in key areas of youth policy; (2) promote youth participation in public affairs; (3) contribute to the active citizenship of young people; (4) promote events that discuss youth issues (such as education and healthy lifestyle); (5) encourage young Europeans to build democratic societies that respect diversity and human rights; (6) create a sense of responsibility for environmental issues; and (7) fight against racism. The main reason that led to the draft of the PI documents was, in fact, the decline in civic and political participation and in the engagement of youngsters. Clearly expressing this central concern, the *Roadmap for Youth* (Presidency of the Portuguese Republic, 2008, p. 2) establishes as a priority

> to stimulate and to enhance the way that young people should participate in a society which is in a deep transformation, becoming an active part of this

change, overcoming the difficulties and anxiety they feel about their responsibility for social renewal.

In the same vein, the Law no. 8/2009 of 18 February, which establishes the legal basis of municipal youth councils, presents a set of objectives that gives young people a greater role in community life, such as: 'to ensure the hearing and representation of public and private entities which, at the municipal level, are related with youth' and 'to encourage and support activities of youth associations, ensuring their representation in municipal bodies, as well as from other public and private, national or foreign entities'.

The NGOs, on the other hand, present a set of projects that bring together a multiplicity of territorial levels, namely local, national, and European. The main objective, for instance, of the Action for Justice and Peace (2008) activity plan is to foster a normative-based discourse around the values of peace and justice 'locally and globally'. The plan's implementation takes place through volunteer work, training opportunities, partnerships with local actors, and institutional support for the creation of small businesses. It seeks to improve the participation and engagement of young people through non-formal mechanisms, and promote the exchange of experiences and good practices of active citizenship among young people. Young people are considered the main actors to be mobilized to achieve these ends, and 'global citizenship' is seen as underpinning the promotion of human development, which has to be sustainable and equitable. Alternative economies and the creation of mechanisms to foster participation and citizenship are also presented in order to achieve socio-economic justice (Action for Justice and Peace, 2008).

Regarding the changes that globalization and modernization have brought about, the National Federation of Youth Associations (FNAJ, 2006) mentions that new approaches and perspectives are necessary to locate young people as social and political actors. The document suggests the implementation of a youth policy that will create conditions for young people's emancipation, countering several obstacles for their successful inclusion such as the crisis of the educational system; the high level of unemployment and precarious jobs; the deregulation of the labour market, which affects the youngsters by converting work (a major element in identity construction) in an element of instability; and the difficulties in obtaining housing and, therefore, the difficulty of an independent life.

Along the same lines, the document of Humana Global (2006) draws attention to the fact that society is experiencing a revolution caused by the development of new information and communication technologies. The sense of identity (with less common values and less shared interests and values than before), the nature of politics, and the ways citizens participate in political processes have changed. Facing these developments and changes, the document suggests that it is necessary to stimulate youth to develop their civic and political participation and their citizenship.

The Portuguese Network of Youth for Equal Opportunities between Women and Men (2006) also presents as its main aim the contribution to the development of more effective participation, specifically in youth organizations. Presenting statistical data regarding the lack of involvement of youth in civic, social, or political groups, it mentions that the low participation of young people is an obstacle to the exercise of their full rights as citizens and leads to political decisions that tend to ignore their specific problems and points of view. The document also stresses that Europe is experiencing a crisis of representation in political and civic life, reflected in a high level of abstention in elections and in low participation in political parties, as well as in other forms of civic and political participation, such as youth associations.

With regard to the European dimension, our sample of both PI and NGO documents contains several references to key priorities and European discourses. Particular emphasis was placed on the promotion of European citizenship based on participatory democracy and the need to improve civic engagement. Important European programmes such as Erasmus, but also 'Youth in Action', are mentioned as essential reference points for building a more cohesive Europe based on the principles of justice and social inclusion which, in turn, are stimulated by mobility and lifelong learning. The documents also stress the importance of promoting positive attitudes towards European identity. The adjective 'European' is used as a reference to the territory, but also to identify a sense of belonging and a set of cultural rights. Therefore, as Humana Global (2006) indicates, when 'European citizenship' is mentioned, it implies not only citizenship but a broader set of values and principles.

Regarding this broader sense of European citizenship, PIs claim they share similar political priorities with the EU, emphasizing that the formative activities developed by the European Council will be maintained by the promotion of the European Youth Campaign 'All different, all equal' for Diversity, and also by the promotion of Human Rights and Participation (National Youth Council, 2007). The *Roadmap for Youth* (Presidency of the Portuguese Republic, 2008) mentions, in addition, that the laws are becoming more European and that European citizenship is gaining autonomy, arguing that the construction of a cohesive Europe, which ensures social justice and responds to the anxieties of today's youth, is the major challenge for the next generations.

In terms of criticisms, NGOs argue that it is really necessary to create policies—at the European and national levels—to support entrepreneurship among local communities. These policies should provide support to certain groups that are sometimes excluded from the labour market—such as youth—with a view to increasing their autonomy. Youth policies should also take into account the position of young people as citizens, providing resources for full-rights citizenship and enabling them to build their own life project and to participate in collective projects. To achieve this goal, the Action for Justice and Peace (2008) proposes that public policies should increase sustainable development through support of alternative and solidarity economies, stressing that political authorities should adopt the Local Agenda 21, a part of Agenda 21. Moreover, the National Federation of Youth Associations (FNAJ, 2006) emphasizes that a new concept of youth requires a new perspective in youth policies, i.e. the recognition of youth as having its own identity, with specific needs and circumstances that demand that public policies take into account their specific reality in relation to adults. In that sense, it suggests that youth policies must overcome elements of generational and institutional paternalism, as well as the 'adultocratic' perspectives that guide them, in order to achieve a more inclusive society, to promote equal rights and duties among all citizens, and to fight situations that may generate processes of social exclusion.

In summary, documents from both sources share significant commonalties in the recommendations for national policy, including the development of inter-institutional networks, the promotion of social inclusion and diversity, and the reinforcement of youth participation. The Constitutional Programme (2009–2013) sums up these ambitions:

> A more developed country involves also instilling young people with democratic and environmental principles and values, of responsibility and social awareness

and of civic and political participation. For this, the Government proposes to: Reinforce citizenship education in personal and social aspects, the curricula of schools and to continue to enhance sexual education, thus promoting awareness and responsibility; Continue to promote and expand programmes of volunteer youth; Promote and support student and youth associations. (Portuguese Constitutional Government, 2009)

Migrants

The dominant discourse in relation to migration has consistently focused on the defence of integration policies. The documents analysed here identify active citizenship organizations and education for citizenship as top priorities. Values such as human rights, solidarity, active citizenship, peace, freedom, and equal rights were widely discussed, especially by NGOs. In this sense, the documents concentrated on the importance of immigration to the Portuguese economy, the rights of migrants in Portuguese society, and their contribution to social and economic growth. In line with this approach, both PIs and NGOs consider it essential to promote social policies that improve the civic and political participation of immigrants and, hence, social inclusion.

Integration policies seek to achieve a level of equality between immigrants and Portuguese citizens and to implement measures that ensure equal opportunities for minorities in general. In this context, the need to establish concrete plans to facilitate the process of integration into the national community is mentioned and linked with factors such as language and other skills considered necessary to ensure and strengthen this process. Additionally, the lack of concrete plans in areas such as unemployment, discrimination, and family policy is identified as particularly problematic and hindering the process of integration. It is in this context that the Plan for the Integration of Immigrants (Presidency of the Council of Ministers, 2007) sought to establish, over three years, a roadmap of concrete commitments that defined the state as the main ally of the integration of immigrants for a more inclusive Portugal. According to the report of the Portuguese High Commissioner for Immigration and Intercultural Dialogue (ACIDI, 2007), the position of Portugal followed the guidelines issued by the multi-annual activities plan of the European Commission. On the legislative and executive realm, 'amendments were made in favour of a more humane society, able to promote the meeting and the coexistence between people with different backgrounds and cultures, an opportunity for building a multicultural and cohesive society' (ACIDI, 2007, p. 9).

Concerning the European dimension, the discourses of the documents, mainly of PIs, focused primarily on pedagogical aspects of education for a European identity and citizenship. Particular attention was paid to the promotion of equal rights and anti-discrimination measures. The Plan for the Integration of Immigrants (Presidency of the Council of Ministers, 2007) argues, for instance, that the demand for higher levels of integration should be consistent, particularly in the areas of employment, social security, housing, health, education and justice, and from a cross-sectoral perspective regarding the issues of racism and discrimination, gender equality, and citizenship. Moreover, participation was widely discussed in the context of European citizenship with a view to promote 'unity in diversity' in order to foster the development of a cultural and civic dimension (AIDGLOBAL, 2009). The European cultural identity, as the NGO Inter-cooperation and Development (2006) states, must be open to other cultures that enter the European space, fostering cultural coexistence and intercultural dialogue.

Regarding NGO-generated counter-discourse, the documents, in general, criticize European immigration policies for not providing sufficient scope for immigrants' economic, social, and cultural rights. More significantly perhaps, they claim that some of them are discriminatory and insufficiently effective. In this regard, the Immigrant Solidarity Association (2007) suggests adjustments in many national and European immigration policies, stating that the problems revealed by those policies should be made public and alternatives should be discussed. Moreover, the report criticizes that some policies imposed by the EU were not sufficiently debated. The EU is thus accused of being oppressive, concerned with secondary issues, and unable to respond to real problems.

In fact, the documents state that integration policies proposed by the EU should be more effective and more equitable between migrant communities, and that the countries of origin of immigrants should be included in the development of European-level programmes (Inter-cooperation and Development, 2006; Institute of Strategic and International Studies, 2009). Issues relating to equality, social exclusion, and marginalization are raised as key problems with the current approach. In this context, policies are therefore seen as failing to provide an adequate framework to address the problems Europe is facing today, often associated with illegal immigration, such as drug trafficking and human trafficking, transnational organized crime, and even terrorism (Institute of Strategic and International Studies, 2009). African migrants are identified as a particularly marginal group. The issue of third-country nationals is discussed as an example of discrimination, since they cannot move freely in the European public space:

> The current immigration policies, guided by security concerns and the exploitation of human beings, criminalize migrants and threaten their human and social rights, both in Europe and Africa (...) The current racist immigration policies do not take into account the real needs of European and African societies and undermine the prospects of sustainable development, both in Europe and Africa. (Immigrant Solidarity Association, 2007)

In general, documents of PIs and NGOs are concerned with the development of practices of active citizenship and the defence of integration policies for both youth and migrants. They are, therefore, in line with the research that points to the low levels of civic and political participation (Benedicto & Morán, 2002; Ferreira, 2006; Perliger et al., 2006; Veiga, 2008; Azevedo, 2009), as well as to the limited access to political rights, especially in the case of immigrants (cf. Carvalhais, 2004, 2006; Zobel & Barbosa, 2009). However, they do not seem to place much emphasis on the 'participatory revolution' that our society is undergoing as young people take on new and more horizontal forms of participation (Norris, 2002; Menezes et al., 2012). This would enable a more critical examination of the current conditions of young people and migrants. On the whole, both PI and NGO documents seem to be aligned with EU political priorities. Notwithstanding, they suggested that integration policies of the EU should be more open to dialogue and debate, i.e. based on the participation of civil society, reinforcing, thus, the idea that EU has an important responsibility in the transformation of societies.

Interviews: Main Findings

NGO Leaders

The priorities mentioned by NGO leaders consist, generally speaking, in defending human rights and promoting the full integration of minority groups at risk of exclusion. To achieve these priorities, they emphasize the importance of denouncing violations of human rights; confronting politicians with their commitments to integrate human rights in policy decisions; influencing people in everyday decisions regarding human rights; increasing people's autonomy and capacity for participation, especially those who are at risk of exclusion; making the relationship between the state and civil society more horizontal, having necessarily at its base public interest; and fighting for new forms of social organization. In addition to these general objectives, it is also important to note that the representative of SOS Racism argues, specifically, that it is a priority to press politicians to legislate on immigrant voting rights, both locally and nationally, as well as to extend adult education (i.e. the 'New Opportunities' programme, aimed at the recognition, validation, and certification of skills) to immigrants:

> SOS will turn twenty and the largest initiative we will develop to mark our twentieth anniversary is a campaign on the voting rights of immigrants, because we understand that ... (t)o be a fully inclusive process, that has to be reflected in the ability of these social agents to be also political agents, to be able to monitor who governs. (SOS Racismo)

Reinforcing the legitimacy of the implementation of these measures, the same interviewee argued that rights are not discrete: if immigrants are citizens then they should have all the rights of a citizen. As he explains:

> The rights are not divisible, not stratified; otherwise the citizen is not a citizen ... To me, that's how I understand it. And the immigration policy has been this, the restriction of rights. (SOS Racismo)

In addition, the representative of Immigrant Solidarity Association also argued that policies should focus on the empowerment of immigrants through the promotion of their rights in order to take advantage of appropriate opportunities to participate: 'If people come in search of a better life, these opportunities should be provided to the people, give them documents to work with rights'.

In relation to European priorities, NGO leaders recognize that the EU has influenced the design of the agenda and the setting of policy priorities at the national level. A representative of the International Solidarity Association stated that the Youth in Action Programme 'is one of the best initiatives at the level of youth that Europe is fostering [...] and had some quite positive effects because it gives youth a chance to rediscover their own citizenship, their own identity'. However, they consider that these policies need to be adapted to the specificities of each country: 'the EU should think in terms of individual countries and not of a one-fits-all program' (Rede ex aequo). They also recognize that there have been many European-level initiatives targeting groups at risk of exclusion, supported by technical and financial resources that have allowed for higher levels of efficiency and sharing of best practices between international partners.

Yet, the assessment NGO leaders make of those initiatives is largely critical of the strategic approach adopted by European bodies, in particular regarding the gap between policy and practice. The representative of Amnesty International is particularly critical of European Commission initiatives on the basis that they are often contradictory, 'because specific policies in the area of cooperation for development indicate a given direction and, after, economic policies point to another'. Moreover, many projects and programmes draw on an artificial European frame in order to obtain European funds:

> (...) there is an increasing tendency for politicians thinking that the problem is solved from the time that there is a law to this effect (...) I also worked a bunch of years in (an NGO) and one of the guidelines that was always imposed was the obligation to give a European dimension to the projects (...) Sometimes these things are very artificial. I recognize the merit and need to give a European dimension to these actions to fight the inconsistency of policies (...) so I think that it is important, but with consistency, with content and not exactly because of funding needs. (Amnesty International)

In a similar vein, a representative of the Immigrant Solidarity Association denounces the lack of political leadership at the European and national levels. The interviewee shows clear opposition to the way that European and Portuguese policy continues to keep thousands of illegal immigrants living without the minimum rights, thus marginalizing these groups further:

> Now, the lack of political courage is huge in European countries and perhaps among almost all political parties (...) The problem arises here because they would lose votes; there are no sincere immigration policies. That's why I say: the attitude of this paradigm has to change. (Solidariedade Imigrante)

Concerning European integration, NGOs are very critical of European political structures and leadership. There is agreement among interviewees that a strong focus on economic drivers undermines European democratic principles and process, and ultimately has a negative impact on the implementation of the human rights agenda (Amnesty International). In this context, the representative of SOS Racism denounces the EU for engaging in *realpolitik* in order to obtain social control, rather than striving to implement ideologically and ethically driven initiatives:

> This is the political cynicism around this discourse because the EU is well aware that immigration is necessary for demographic and socio-economic reasons, but at the same time they have to do a bit of *realpolitik* to calm down the public opinion because there is a feeling of invasion. (SOS Racismo)

Given the criticisms, it is suggested that the EU should specifically revoke the 'Return Directive' and proceed to the legalization of all undocumented immigrants. As the representative of the Immigrant Solidarity Association points out, the European directive is the 'Directive of Shame', 'the Directive that criminalizes immigration'. Supporting this, the representative of SOS Racism argues that:

> Europe does not have to chase hegemonic arrogance. Europe has to worry about creating a model that is an example for all (...) for the entire planet, which is a different social model, based on peace, dialogue, culture. Europe has always been a light and it's in this that Europe has to invest. (SOS Racismo)

On the whole, NGO leaders criticize the lack of political leadership at the European and national levels in order to implement policies for the development of an effective active citizenship and for the integration of groups at risk of exclusion. At the same time, the interviewees reveal that NGOs have difficulty in being represented and in taking part in agenda-setting processes at the EU level, criticizing the vertical relationship between EU bodies and NGOs. In this context, an analysis of interviews suggests that the engagement and accessibility of national NGOs in the supranational arenas should be improved.

Policy Makers

Like NGO leaders, the priorities presented by policy makers focus primarily on the full integration of migrants and other minorities, based on an intercultural model that respects diversity. The following excerpt illustrates well what has been the priority for the Portuguese ACIDI:

> No doubt that the priority is to do everything for migrants to be fully integrated (...) always respecting the culture of immigrants but also interacting with them and growing with this relationship of openness to the other. And, therefore, different strategies have been designed to make this happen through direct contact, including through national centres to support immigrants, local centres, network offices for employment and immigrant associations (...) also at the level of awareness-raising. In addition, our immigration observatory enables studying all the issues related to immigrants to help define public policies for their integration. (ACIDI)

In a similar vein, a representative of the National Action Plan for Social Inclusion (PNAI) emphasizes that discrimination, poverty, and lack of access to education, training, and qualifications must be overcome in order to strengthen the integration of specific groups at risk of exclusion. To achieve these priorities she suggested increasing social and political awareness as this will foster a sense of empowerment and ownership:

> First, distributing the right information and the right information is information that is accessible to people, which speaks the language that they speak, etc. Then, working also as a space of resonance regarding what people say and also as a place of influence. (PNAI)

The policy makers' discourses reveal that state institutions have an important role in the promotion of full integration of groups at risk of exclusion. However, they recognize that this task has not been always effectively implemented, suggesting the difficulty in matching the prescribed political discourses with real life.

Elected members of the Portuguese parliament provide an interesting insight into the political priorities and the nature of debate that frames policy development within state institutions. The Member of Parliament interviewed for this project highlighted the hierarchical nature of agenda-setting processes. The immediate problems arising from the current financial and economic crisis are deemed to be a higher political priority than any other social policy matters. The discourse about young people is framed in terms of their potential contribution to the economy. The focus is on providing this group with a set of tools that will enable them to become active members of the labour market. Political and civic participation are seen as deriving from participation in the economy.

Unfortunately, this is a highly commodified view of citizenship and participation, which ultimately limits the scope and quality of participation and engagement. It is, however, aligned with the European model of citizenship. The view that Portugal should align with European norms and guidelines is a common theme in all interviews. In particular, they point to the impact and importance of the EU's work to guide and standardize social policy frameworks in the member states.

The development of EU projects related to the integration of minorities is considered especially important in a time of crisis, as it contributes to the maintenance of European identity as a space that promotes human rights and equality. Although policy makers recognize a positive role of the EU in promoting civic and political participation and in the integration of groups at risk of exclusion, they, like the NGOs, also stress the diversity of national realities and point to the need to adapt these projects to the requirements of each Member State. Lack of adequate resources is identified as an obstacle to the delivery of the European project's stated objectives. The European social dimension comes to the forefront of this critique; this policy area is largely seen as losing out to higher economic imperatives framing the wider political agenda:

> We are in a situation, clearly, of a much more modest commitment to social issues which, interestingly, happens in coincidence with the arrival of Eastern countries (...) When the revision of (the Lisbon Treaty) was proposed in 2005, clearly the social dimension was dropped and we began to identify the social dimension with employment, which is, in fact, an impoverishment of the social dimension. (PNAI)

Finally, those working at the European level highlight the failure of the Constitutional Treaty in 2005, arguing that weak negotiations culminated in a restrictive vision of the role of the EU in social affairs. The negotiations—and the ensuing Treaty—were too narrowly concentrated on economic issues. This focus consolidated the position of those opposing further integration. The rise of Euro-sceptic movements and the establishment of a dominant discourse about the EU's role in eroding national sovereignty and independence are perceived to be the result of the negotiations. In this context, policy makers also add that the EU used to be more democratic than it is today. They acknowledge that this is likely to be the result of the economic crisis and of a shift in political culture in many Member States. Increasing opposition to immigration is seen to be a direct result of this wider political and economic context:

> Europe has been more democratic than it is now, perhaps because of the crisis (...). In some countries there begin to emerge antidemocratic movements that concern me, and looking at our Europe, which always wanted to be humanist, democratic, concerned with the human person (...). (ACIDI)

Despite criticizing the Treaties for adopting a rationale imposed by economic imperatives, policy makers view the Lisbon Treaty as an important step for the development of the EU. It is seen as an opportunity to build a more robust strategy in relation to the global competition that characterizes the world today. However, it is suggested that civil society should be more involved in the design of policies and that, accordingly, the Lisbon Treaty should have been subject to a referendum 'because this way, this discussion, the involvement, and the creation of movements would have led to a more intense discussion and to an increasing assimilation of what is Europe' (Member of Parliament).

It is interesting to note the convergence in the position of government officials and civil society organizations on this particular issue. Both NGO leaders and policy makers are very critical of the ways that policies have been implemented at the EU level. In effect, they stress that it is important to overcome the hegemony of economic factors and promote a greater involvement of civil society in policy decisions in order to enhance EU democracy.

Conclusion

Regarding perceptions of civil society, as seen in the document analysis, what stands out is the existence of a strong concern to align national policy priorities with those established by supranational entities coordinated by the EU. Moreover, this search for aligning political priorities contributes most probably to the positive evaluations that several international organizations have been making of immigration policies in Portugal. For instance, the report of the United Nations Development Programme (2009) gave Portugal the best score regarding immigrants' access to rights and services. The International Organization for Migration (2010) points out Portugal as a model in terms of the relationship with immigrants, who are actively involved in a dialogue concerning integration policy. Finally, the Migrant Integration Policy Index III (British Council and Migration Policy Group, 2011, p. 29) concludes that 'Portugal goes further than other new countries of immigration in the promotion of social integration in education'.

Despite the positive international assessments of Portuguese policies, NGO leaders and policy makers tend to criticize the ways they have been implemented. In this context, a crucial notion is that there is no consistent match between the policies' objectives and the effects that civil society believes they have or can have. Thus, it was stressed that there is need to adopt a strategy that can bridge the gap between the prescribed and the real, as well as the importance of overcoming the hegemony of economic factors in policy decisions. This notion resonates with previous research emphasizing the importance of promoting access to political rights (cf. Carvalhais, 2004, 2006; Zobel & Barbosa, 2009) and the relationship between policy and practice, a phenomenon that is recurrent in research with immigrants and other groups at risk of exclusion (Loja *et al.*, 2011; Ribeiro *et al.*, 2012): despite positive changes that have occurred in the last few years, there is still an important gap between policy and practice (Ribeiro *et al.*, 2012).

Furthermore, NGO leaders criticize the lack of political courage because the EU continues to keep thousands of illegal immigrants living without the minimum rights, as well the cynicism of politicians and policies (*realpolitik*) grounded in demographic and economic reasons. In this respect, they propose the revocation of the 'Return Directive' and the implementation of policies focused on the empowerment of immigrants through the effective promotion of their rights. Regarding European identity and integration,

NGO leaders criticize the vertical relationship between the EU and the NGOs, which undermines civil society and the functioning of the democracy, arguing that Europe must be collectively constructed. In addition, policy makers highlight that the failure of the Constitutional Treaty in 2005 resulted from a weak negotiation process.

Overall, both document analysis and interviews present as dominant discourses the need to increase the civic and political participation of youth and to achieve the full integration of migrants. In relation to youth, the discourses seem to focus on the social and civil rights level, emphasizing the importance of providing more and equal opportunities, especially in education and in the labour market, enhancing their autonomy and encouraging their active citizenship. Regarding immigrants, the discourses were mostly located in the realm of political rights, which resonates once again with what has been emphasized in the literature (Zobel & Barbosa, 2009). The implementation of less bureaucratic policies promoting the legalization of migrants is seen as a priority to be established in national and EU policy. The objective is to promote their effective participation towards full integration in society, in order to overcome the distance between official discourses and actual practices. Indeed, this concern was already pointed out in a previous study regarding the evaluation of the Portuguese legislation by civil society (e.g. NGOs, immigrant associations, churches, as well as political parties and governmental officials) and the political integration of non-national residents, stressing that the problem is not the law but its application. Furthermore, although the discourses are aligned with EU political priorities, they point to the need to improve the representation and participation of civil society in agenda-setting at the EU level, and criticize the hegemony of economic factors over the social dimension in the political agenda.

Concluding, this article has sought to contribute to a better understanding of the factors that influence the active citizenship of youth and migrants. The analysis was focused on the interaction between state institutions and civil society actors, addressing the role of national and EU policies on the integration of youth and migrants. In line with the literature, the analysis reinforces the idea that political opportunity structures play an important role in civic and political participation (cf. Koopmans, 2004; Morales, 2009). Despite this important influence over active citizenship, especially for those groups at risk of exclusion, the analysis shows that some sectors of society have been ignored in the formulation of policies, which may indicate that there is a lack of capabilities and political courage in both national and European institutions to endorse legal and political innovations to effectively improve their political integration (cf. Zobel & Barbosa, 2009). In this context, it is suggested that it is necessary to promote a greater involvement of civil society in the design and implementation of policies which, in turn, may contribute to the strengthening of the democratic principles in which Portugal and the European Community are grounded. In other words, and to use the metaphor of one of the interviewees, *Europe has always been a beacon pointing* towards the enlargement of citizenship rights and the inclusion of disenfranchised groups—and, more than ever, European institutions should recognize that the quality of democracy in the EU also depends on their leadership in the creation and development of more inclusive and participatory ways of being a citizen.

Acknowledgements

The data presented here were collected by the Portuguese team of PIDOP, a multinational research project supported by a grant received from the European Commission 7th

Framework Programme, FP7-SSH-2007-1, Grant Agreement n°: 225282, *Processes Influencing Democratic Ownership and Participation (PIDOP)* awarded to the University of Surrey (UK), University of Liège (Belgium), Masaryk University (Czech Republic), University of Jena (Germany), University of Bologna (Italy), University of Porto (Portugal), Örebro University (Sweden), Ankara University (Turkey) and Queen's University Belfast (UK). Norberto Ribeiro is supported with a PhD grant by the Portuguese Foundation of Science and Technology (FCT) (SFRH/BD/78506/2011). Carla Malafaia is supported with a PhD grant by the Portuguese Foundation of Science and Technology (FCT) (SFRH/BD/92113/2012). Maria Fernandes-Jesus is supported with a PhD grant by the Portuguese Foundation of Science and Technology (FCT) (SFRH/BD/62567/2009).

Notes

1. Approved by the European Parliament (2008/115/EC) with the aim of being the first step towards a common immigration policy for the EU, establishing common standards and procedures in Member States for returning illegally staying third-country nationals:
2. As suggested by the notion of post-national citizenship by Carvalhais (2006, p. 118), the concept of integration is perceived in this article as a process by which the individuals became active participants in their economic, civic, political, cultural, and spiritual life for the exercise of their citizenship.
3. Law 50/1996 of 4 September (art. 1(b)).
4. See Barrett and Brunton-Smith (2014) in this issue.
5. Available at the website: http://ec.europa.eu/youth/policy/eu-youth-strategy_en.htm

References

ACIDI (High Commissioner for Immigration and Intercultural Dialogue). (2007) *Activities Report 2007*. Available at http://www.acidi.gov.pt/_cfn/4d346bd641db7/live/Relat%C3%B3rio+de+Actividades+do+ACIDI+%282007%29 (accessed 1 December 2009).
Action for Justice and Peace. (2008) *The Future Is not an Improvement of the Present: It Is Something Else. Annual Activities Plan—2008*. Available at http://www.ajpaz.org.pt (accessed 30 November 2009).
Ahmad, N. & Pinnock, K. (2007) *Civic Participation: Potential Differences Between Ethnic Groups* (London: Commission for Racial Equality).
AIDGLOBAL—Action and Integration for Local Development. (2009) *Activities Plan for 2009*. Available at http://www.aidglobal.org/userfiles/files/plano_actividades/plano_actividades_2009.pdf (accessed 30 November 2009).
Azevedo, M. C. (2009) Experiências de participação dos jovens: um estudo longitudinal sobre a influência da qualidade da participação no desenvolvimento psicológico, Unpublished doctoral dissertation, University of Porto, Porto, Portugal, 2009.
Barrett, M. & Brunton-Smith, I. (2014) Political and civic engagement and participation: Towards an integrative approach, *Journal of Civil Society*. doi: 10.1080/17448689.2013.871911
Benedicto, J. & Morán, M. L. (2002) *La construcción de una ciudadanía activa entre los jóvenes* (Madrid: Instituto de la Juventud).
Benhabib, S. (1999) Citizens, residents and aliens in a changing world: Political member-ship in a global era, *Social Research*, 66(3), pp. 709–744.
British Council & Migration Policy Group. (2011). *Migrant Integration Policy Index III Portugal* (Brussels: British Council & Migration Policy Group). Available at http://www.mipex.eu/sites/default/files/downloads/portugal_abridged_migrant_integration_policy_index_mipexiii_2011_pt.pdf (accessed 29 July 2011).
Carvalhais, I. E. (2004) *Os Desafios da Cidadania Pós-Nacional* (Porto: Afrontamento).
Carvalhais, I. E. (2006) Condição Pós-nacional da Cidadania Política: Pensar a integração de residentes não-nacionais em Portugal. *Sociologia, Problemas e Práticas*, 50, pp. 109–130.

Ferreira, P. D. (2006) Concepções de cidadania e experiências de participação na sociedade civil: uma perspectiva do desenvolvimento psicológico, Unpublished doctoral dissertation, University of Porto, Porto, Portugal, 2006.

FNAJ (National Federation of Youth Associations). (2006) *Public Policies for Youth. Program of Youth Association Movement*. Available at http://www.fajdg.org/images/Conc_8ENAJ.pdf (accessed 4 January 2010).

Geddes, A. (2000) *Immigration and European Integration. Towards Fortress Europe?* (Manchester: Manchester University Press).

Grassi, M. (2007) Práticas, Formas e Solidariedades da integração de jovens de origem angolana no mercado de trabalho em Portugal, *Economia Global e Gestão*, 12(3), pp. 71–91.

Grassi, M. (2009) *Capital social e jovens originários dos PALOP em Portugal* (Lisboa: Imprensa de Ciências Sociais).

Hajer, M. A. (2002) Discourse analysis and the study of policy making, *European Political Science*, 2(1), pp. 61–65.

Hajer, M. A. (2005) Coalitions, practices, and meaning in environmental politics: From acid rain to BSE, in: D. Howarth & J. Torfing (Eds) *Discourse Theory in European Politics. Identity, Policy and Governance*, pp. 297–315 (Houndmills: Palgrave).

Harris, A., Wyn, J. & Younes, S. (2010) Beyond apathetic or activist youth: 'Ordinary' young people and contemporary forms of participation, *Young*, 18(1), pp. 9–32.

Hooghe, M. (2005) Ethnic organizations and social movement theory: The political opportunity structure for ethnic mobilisation in Flanders, *Journal of Ethnic and Migration Studies*, 31(5), pp. 833–864.

Howarth, D. & Torfing, J. (Eds) (2005) *Discourse Theory in European Politics. Identity, Policy and Governance* (Houndmills: Palgrave).

Humana Global. (2006) *Under Construction: Citizenship, Youth and Europe. Training Kit N° 7*. Available at http://www.publicacoeshumanas.org/download/t-kit7.pdf (accessed 30 November 2009).

Immigrant Solidarity Association (Association for Immigrants' Rights Defence). (2007) *Activities and Evaluation Report—2007*. Available at http://www.solimigrante.org/wp-content/uploads/2008/11/relatorio-actividades-2007.pdf (accessed 30 November 2009).

Institute of Strategic and International Studies. (2009) *Immigration, Integration and Diversity. What Are the European Responses?* Available at http://ftp.infoeuropa.eurocid.pt/database/000042001-000043000/000042746.pdf (accessed 4 January 2010).

Inter-cooperation and Development (INDE). (2006) *Activities Report 2006*. Available at http://www.inde.pt (accessed 30 November 2009).

International Organization for Migration. (2010) *World Migration Report 2010. The Future of Migration: Building Capacities for Change* (Geneva: International Organization for Migration).

Ireland, P. (1994) *The Policy Challenge of Ethnic Diversity: Immigrant Politics in France and Switzerland* (Cambridge, MA: Harvard University Press).

Janoski, T. (2000) *Citizenship and Civil Society: A Framework of Rights and Obligations in Liberal, Traditional and Social Democratic Regimes* (Cambridge: Cambridge University Press).

Juris, J. S. & Pleyers, G. H. (2009) Alter-activism: Emerging cultures of participation among young global justice activists, *Journal of Youth Studies*, 12(1), pp. 57–75.

Koopmans, R. (2004) Migrant mobilisation and political opportunities: Variation among German cities and a comparison with the United Kingdom and the Netherlands, *Journal of Ethnic and Migration Studies*, 30(3), pp. 449–470.

Koopmans, R. & Statham, P. (2000) Migration and ethnic relations as a field of political contention: An opportunity structure approach, in: R. Koopmans & P. Statham (Eds) *Challenging Immigration and Ethnic Relations Politics. Comparative European Perspectives*, pp. 14–56 (Oxford: Oxford University Press).

Loja, E., Costa, M. E. & Menezes, I. (2011) Views of disability in Portugal: 'Fado' or citizenship? *Disability & Society*, 26(5), pp. 567–581.

Lopez, M. H. & Marcelo, K. B. (2008) The civic engagement of immigrant youth: New evidence from the 2006 civic and political health of the nation survey, *Applied Developmental Science*, 12(2), pp. 66–73.

Magalhães, P. & Moral, J. S. (2008) *Os jovens e a política: um estudo do Centro de Sondagens e Estudos de Opinião da Universidade Católica Portuguesa* (CESOP: Catholic University of Portugal).

Marques, M. M. & Santos, R. (2004) Welfare and immigrants' inclusion in a context of weak civil society: Associations and local politics in Oeiras, in: F. Eckardt & D. Hassenpflug (Eds) *Urbanism and Globalization*, pp. 107–129 (Frankfurt: Peter Lang Publishers).

Marsh, D., O'Toole, T. & Jones, S. (2007) *Young People and Politics in the UK: Apathy or Alienation?* (London: Palgrave).

Menezes, I., Afonso, R., Gião, J. & Amaro, G. (Org.). (2005) *Conhecimentos, concepções e práticas de cidadania dos jovens portugueses: Um estudo internacional* (Lisboa: DGIDC).

Menezes, I., Ribeiro, N., Fernandes-Jesus, M., Malafaia, C. & Ferreira, P. D. (2012) *Agência e Participação Cívica e Política: Jovens e Imigrantes na Construção da Democracia* (Porto: Livpsic/Legis Editora).

Morales, L. (2009) *Joining Political Organisations: Institutions, Mobilisation and Participation in Western Democracies* (Colchester: ECPR Press).

National Youth Council (CNJ). (2007) *Activities Plan 2007*. Available at http://www.cnj.pt/site/ (accessed 30 November 2009).

Norris, P. (2002) *Democratic Phoenix: Reinventing Political Activism* (Cambridge: Cambridge University Press).

Perliger, A., Canetti-Nisim, D. & Pedahzur, A. (2006) Democratic attitudes among high-school pupils: The role played by perceptions of class climate, *School Effectiveness and School Improvement*, 17(1), pp. 119–140.

Portuguese Constitutional Government. (2009) *XVIII Constitutional Government Program 2009–2013*. Available at http://www.portugal.gov.pt/pt/o-governo/arquivo-historico/governos-constitucionais/gc18/programa-do-governo/programa-do-governo-constitucional-18.aspx (accessed 4 January 2010).

Portuguese Network of Young People for Equality of Opportunities Between Women and Men. (2006). *Girls and Boys in Youth Organizations: A Guide for Gender Mainstreaming*. Available at http://www.redejovensigualdade.org.pt/dmpm1/docs/guia-mainstreaming-genero.pdf (accessed 11 February 2010).

Presidency of the Council of Ministers. (2007) *Resolution of the Council of Ministers n° 63-A/2007—Plan for the Integration of Immigrants*. Available at http://www.acidi.gov.pt/_cfn/4d346c9b80687/live/Resolu%C3%A7%C3%A3o+de+Conselho+de+Ministros+n.%C2%BA+63-A%2F2007,+de+3+de+Maio (accessed 18 February 2010).

Presidency of the Portuguese Republic. (2008) *Roadmap for Youth—1st Journey: Autonomy of Young People and of Youth Associations*. Available at http://www.presidencia.pt/archive/doc/Roteiro_para_a_Juventude_-_1__Jornada_-_Enquadramento.pdf (accessed 4 January 2010).

Putnam, R. D. (2000) *Bowling Alone: The Collapse and Revival of American Community* (New York: Simon & Schuster).

Ribeiro, N., Malafaia, C., Fernandes-Jesus, M., Neves, T., Ferreira, P. & Menezes, I. (2012) Education and citizenship: Redemption or disempowerment? A study of Portuguese-speaking migrant (and non-migrant) youth in Portugal, *Power and Education*, 4(2), pp. 207–218.

Sardinha, J. (2007) Providing voices? Civic participation opportunities for immigrants in Portugal, *POLITIS Working Paper 7*, University of Oldenburg, Oldenburg.

Schrover, M. & Vermeulen, F. (2005) Immigrant organizations, *Journal of Ethnic and Migration Studies*, 31(5), pp. 823–832.

Soysal, Y. (1994) *Limits of Citizenship. Migrants and Postnational Membership in Europe* (Chicago: The University of Chicago).

Teixeira, A. & Albuquerque, R. (2005) *Active Civic Participation of Immigrants in Portugal*, Report Prepared for the European Research Project POLITIS, Oldenburg: University of Oldenburg.

Veiga, C. S. M. (2008) O impacto do envolvimento dos estudantes universitários em actividades extra-curriculares no empowerment e no desenvolvimento cognitivo-vocacional, Unpublished doctoral dissertation, University of Porto, Porto, Portugal, 2008.

United Nations Development Programme. (2009) *Human Development Report 2009. Overcoming Barriers: Human Mobility and Developments*. Available at http://hdr.undp.org/en/media/HDR_2009_EN_Complete.pdf (accessed 8 November 2010).

Zobel, C. & Barbosa, C. E. (2009) Aproximación á participación formal de cidadáns dos países lusófonos na política local portuguesa, *Tempo exterior*, X(I)(19), pp. 47–60.

Zukin, C., Keeter, S., Andolina, M., Jenkins, K. & Delli Carpini, M. X. (2006) *A New Engagement? Political Participation, Civic Life, and the Changing American Citizen* (New York: Oxford University Press).

Civic and Political Participation of Women and Youth in Turkey: An Examination of Perspectives of Public Authorities and NGOs

TULIN SENER

Faculty of Educational Sciences, Ankara University, Ankara, Turkey

ABSTRACT *The aim of this article is to present a review of the discourses of public authorities and non-governmental organizations (NGOs) on civic and political participation of youth and women in Turkey. Drawing on policy documents and elite interviews, this article explores the role of civil society organizations in promoting civic and political organizations in traditionally marginal groups. The article is primarily concerned with unpacking dominant discourses, as produced by public documents and official statements by both civil society organizations and policy-makers. The analysis will produce an overview of their general discursive orientations and the related legal changes and policy implementations. The article then looks at the impact of these discursive formulations to the issue of participation. What is important to note is that action plans and strategies are not always implemented in a manner that is in keeping with the original intentions of policy-makers. The review of public and civil society documents highlights serious differences in focus and coverage between the groups. It also highlights limited engagement with the actual issues of civic and political participation. While youth participation is paid limited attention, women participation is mostly associated with political representation in national and local political bodies.*

Introduction

Civic and political participation are composed of a variety of activities in Turkey. Whereas women have traditionally been excluded to a great extent from formal and informal participation, youths have been portrayed as an 'apolitical' category whose political engagement can be regarded as destabilizing or 'dangerous'.[1] This perspective has also been embedded in Turkish youth services and policies, which have almost exclusively been limited to sports and leisure activities. This approach has much to do with the role of the military in shaping the political history of the country, e.g. the 1960 Coup, followed by a Memorandum in 1971, a coup in 1980 and an intervention in 1997. Although there have been different causes for the political turmoil, these 'interventions' into the governance of the country have had a negative impact on individuals/citizens' attitudes towards participation and civic engagement. In this regard, the 1980 Coup and the Constitution codified by the military junta in 1982 can be seen as critical junctures in relation to the issues addressed in this article. The of regime's hostility against a variety of political activities culminated in the inclusion of restrictive measures in the Constitution and associated secondary legislation. As indicated by Enneli (2011, p. 264) strict antidemocratic control mechanisms established by the 1982 Constitution have shaped young people's perceptions and (negative) attitudes towards politics and can account for widespread 'depoliticization' in the country. This is also true for the women, whose civic and political involvements have historically been limited due to factors such as conservative social norms and traditional roles within the family. Although there are specific amendments dealing with the general situations of youth and women in Turkey, which directly or indirectly have shaped the political participation of these groups (for a more detailed discussion see Seckinelgin, 2006, pp. 753–754), it can be argued that the civic and political participation have hardly been a prominent concern for the policy-makers. The limited number of available documents seeking to address or introduce policies for youth and women can also be seen as being indicative of the lack of wider trends and attitudes within the political structures and environment of the country.

The aim of this article is to present a review of the discourses of public authorities and non-governmental organizations (NGOs) on civic and political participation of youth and women in Turkey by leaning upon the policy documents reviewed and the interviews made within the scope of the PIDOP Project.[2] Throughout the PIDOP Project, a distinction has been made for the meanings of civic and political participation as well as participation and engagement. Barrett (2011) assumes that *participation* is an activity that is a 'good for community' building or has a direct impact on governance. Engagement on the other hand is seen as a psychological process relating to individuals' opinions or values about a social issue. Adopting Verba *et al.*'s (1995, p. 37) definition of political particiaption whereby it is seen as an opportunity to communicate concerns and preferences to the authorities, Zani and Barrett (2012) and Pachi and Barrett (2012) describe it as an effective way for influencing governance, either directly (by affecting the making or implementation of public policy) or indirectly (by influencing the selection of individuals who make that policy). In this context, political participation can take different forms; it can adhere to conventional norms such as taking part in the electoral processes (voting, election campaigning, and running for election), or it can take on non-conventional practices (e.g. signing petitions, participating in political demonstrations, displaying a symbol or sign representing support for a political cause, membership of political campaigning organizations, writing letters to politicians and public officials, etc.). Civic participation, on the other hand, is defined as a voluntary activity focused on helping others, achieving a public good or solving a community problem (Zukin *et al.*, 2006), including work undertaken either alone or in cooperation with others in order to effect change. Ekman and Amnå (2012) developed a new typology to help clarify the difference between 'civic engagement' and 'political participation'. Their typology brings together different forms, attitudes and behaviour in order to account for participation at the individual and collective level. According to Zani and Barrett (2012), the typology is important in terms of incorporating a non-participation category which is further divided in order to account for individuals who are apolitical as opposed to antipolitical. The analysis of non-participation allows for the introduction of the concept of 'stand-by citizen' (i.e. a person who is engaged with and shows interest in politics but who does not actually participate), thus going beyond the conventional active/passive dichotomy (Zani & Barrett, 2012).

Key part of the PIDOP project was the analysis of current policies on participation. This work sought to identify and assess dominant policy discourses about civic and political participation at the European, national, and regional levels. The project focused on traditionally marginal groups (i.e. youth, women, minorities, and migrants); one of the main research questions was to compare these groups at the national level in order to establish similarities and differences in the processes leading to engagement and participation. The overall aim was to understand the relevant policy contexts. This was important so as to develop and recommend strategies and policies on the effecting groups, particularly on youth and women. The analysis of key policies provides the backdrop for understanding individual pathways to engagement. The project examined a number of policy documents and follow-up interviews were conducted with policy-makers and representatives of national NGOs working in this field.

So, this paper attempts to provide an examination of a dimension of civic and political participation in Turkey. For this particular case, the project analysed 32 documents produced between 2004 and 2011 by related public authorities and NGOs. In addition to this six follow-up interviews were conducted to gain a more detailed understanding of the peculiarities of the Turkish socio-political system, key government priorities, the emergence of counter discourses, and the role of civil society in promoting alternative forms of political participation. Identifying and examining these perspectives is necessary for contextualizing the dynamics of participation, that is to say, for taking into account the impact of civic and political environments. Simply put, this article looks at how the Turkish policy environment framed women and youth participation, as framed by the documents analysed here. The first consideration to be made relates to the overall quality of the document produced. One of the main challenges for this project was to find suitable documents that would articulate a clear youth policy in Turkey. This can be considered as an important factor showing that little attention is given to this issue, despite the large proportion of the population under the age of 25. It was assumed at the beginning that the analysis of basic discourses in policy documents would lead us to the identification of political priorities on women and youth and their impact on policy outcomes.

Given the fact that there are a variety of youth and women NGOs in Turkey having different perspectives and approaches, the documents and the interviews included in the study are not claimed to be representative. While the interviews were incorporated as supplementary materials in the study, the documents were selected as a result of a review of the official websites of youth and women organizations reached via the NGO Database of the Civil Society Development Centre.[3] All relevant documents released by these NGOs in their official web sites are included. The next section of this article provides a historical and conceptual overview of civic and political participation in Turkey. This framework is then applied to the analysis of civil society's documents in order to understand their perspectives on women and youth participation. Finally, the concluding section outlines the key findings and main trends shaping participation and engagement of traditionally marginal groups in contemporary Turkey.

Civic and Political Participation in Turkey: A Historical and Conceptual Overview

As a country with a troubled political history, Turkey has struggled to establish a positive environment that promotes citizens' civic and political participation in general. Women and youth have been categories that also deserve special attention in that respect. Although the right to vote and be elected was granted to women in Turkey in 1934, rather early compared to many European cases, their political representation has remained highly restricted. Furthermore, despite the increasing number of women active in civic and political life, there seems to be a considerable gap between those who are actively engaging in the social, economic, and political life of the country and the majority for whom politics remains a distant reality (Çelik & Lüküslü, 2012, p. 31). In addition to this, women's participation has historically focused on issues of equality such as domestic violence, restricted participation in education, and labour force. The politicization of these issues at the hands of women's organization led to significant changes and developments in the country. As indicated by Ayata and Tütüncü (2008, p. 365), feminist movements, both by their demands and their infiltration into the political parties and other political movements, have had an important place within the political landscape in Turkey in the last couple of decades. This trend has also been accompanied by important (although limited) legal changes on key issues affecting women's social, political, and economic status. A detailed analysis of these changes highlights key differences in the way the government and civil society organizations seek to represent women's interests in the public sphere. Whereas the government's approach tends to be 'family oriented', feminist organizations tend to take a 'women-oriented' approach. In this context, the establishment of a ministry under the name of 'Ministry of Family and Social Policies (MoFSP)' in 2011 and the placement of the 'General Directorate on the Status of Women' under the roof of this ministry implies that women are mainly treated as 'family members' by public authorities. As such, issues related to women as members of households and/or mothers seem to be prioritized, which is not the same as promoting a 'women-centred' agenda.

Youth participation and engagement also deserve special attention in Turkey, as this age group makes up a large proportion of the country's population. According to 2011 data youths (i.e. individuals between 15 and 24 years of age) make up 16.8% of the total population, this corresponds to approximately 12.5 million individuals (TSI, 2012, p. 16). It is interesting to note that despite the large youth base in the country, comprehensive strategies and policies that specifically target youth participation are few and far in between. Yet there are some recent developments which have the potential to increase youth's political and civic engagement. Perhaps a turning point in Turkey's approach to youth policy was the establishment of the Ministry of Youth and Sports in 2011 (which used to be the General Directorate of Youth and Sports). The restructuring of youth services and policies under a government ministry, with a larger budget, should lead to the establishment of comprehensive youth policies. That said, the Ministry's focus on sports and leisure in relation to youth policies is a serious limitation in its ability to engage with youths in a meaningful and mature way. It will likely prove to be a constraining force on the establishment of a wider policy agenda seeking to address youth-related issues and problems. One of the recent projects undertaken by this Ministry is to prepare a youth policy to set out the government's strategy; this project is ongoing with little evidence of progress to date.

One of the key developments in youth policy worthy of note here is the establishment of 'youth centres', with remit for providing entry points for youth work activities, training and personal development, and planning. Clearly, the focus of many of these activities is employability and training. These activities are coordinated by the Ministry and thus contribute to the delivery of the government's policy agenda. Besides, the appropriateness of the activities to the actual needs of the young people, transparency and the level of youth participation has still been a question mark. Even though the target audience for youth centres is youth, some of these activities were designed without the participation of young people. As indicated by the geographical distribution of organizations, which receive support from the National Agency[4] or from the Ministry, youth services have not reached all parts of Turkey. Young people from rural areas have more obstacles to access information and opportunities. Recently, Eurodesk operating under the National Agency has started to work on youth information support in order to disseminate information about existing opportunities more effectively, especially to those who reside in disadvantaged regions of the country.

Turkey, being a part of the Convention on the Rights of the Children, has ratified several regulations to support young citizens under the age of 18. Children's courts have been developed and laws adopted in adherence to the Convention. In terms of protection, the social security department has established Child Police units to tackle issues related to children's welfare. There are several regulations in terms of protecting the rights of the children, which can be considered as positive developments. The main problem, however, remains the formal implantation of these policies. For instance, many of the judges assigned to the children's courts area are drawn from the criminal justice system. This means that the judges do not necessarily have the skills to deal with the emotional complexity of the issues coming in front of the court. The main focus seems to be on protecting society from the young people who had engaged in criminal activities. In addition to the Ministry of Youth and Sports, MoFSP is also responsible for developing and implementing policies related to disadvantaged youths. Turkey is currently increasing its investment in social services, but the quality and the relevance of the implementation are rather weak and insufficient. The approach and the capacity of the organization are not developed enough to address the needs of young people in a way to integrate such young people in to society.

Alongside these developments that would potentially enhance youth participation in an indirect manner, there is also a recent attempt to decrease the age of candidacy in national elections to 18. At the time of writing, the debate about introducing a formal amendment to improve access to political structures and about whether it would actually increase youth political participation is still ongoing. Article 58 of the Constitution outlines very clearly the way in which the state views youths as citizens. According to this article, the future of the Republic is entrusted to this group, as opposed to other sections of society defined within the Constitution, such as women, people with disabilities, or citizens. The state's obligation is to take precautions to ensure the 'training' and 'development' of youth. However, the fundamental aim of this 'training' and 'development' is to oppose 'ideas aiming at the destruction of the indivisible integrity of the state with its territory and nation'. Furthermore, 'precautions' are to be taken for the fundamental objective of securing the continuity and the unity of the state. Hence, the main focus of this section of Article 58 does not seek to support youths per se, but rather it outlines the extent to which state intervention in the affairs of youth can be legitimized in order to minimize the potential 'harm' that may be brought to the state by means of youth. Therefore, these 'precautions' are in favour of the state and are conceptualized in terms of the state's right to intervene and protect, rather than the rights and needs of the youth.

Perspectives of Public Authorities and NGOs on Women and Youth Civic and Political Participation

Women

The examination of policy documents and interviews realized within the scope of this study implies that as a general tendency, women's participation is regarded by political authorities and by some NGOs mostly within the confines of the conventional forms of participation and especially the political representation in the parliament and local politics. In parallel with this and given the acute problems of women in Turkey such as domestic violence, poverty and limited education, the attention seems to be directed towards these issues, and civic and political participation are deemed secondary. The lack of a considerable reference to the issues related to participation in the documents produced by public authorities in relation to women in Turkey also implies this secondary character. An important exception to this can be regarded as the 2008–2013 Action Plan produced by the 'General Directorate on the Status of Women', which determines political participation as one of the priorities of the organization and emphasizes that:

> Objectives of development and modernity cannot be achieved without an active participation of women in all levels of decision-making and management since in those positions of power decisions are taken that affect the whole society. More women in powerful positions mean more effective solutions for the problems and needs of female citizens. (KSGM, 2008, p. 47)

Yet, despite the institution's emphasis on active participation in all levels of decision-making, the main focus of the Action Plan in relation to participation remains within the confines of the conventional forms of political participation such as the representation of women in the national and local elections and in the top positions in the public and private sector, judiciary, academia, and trade unions (KSGM, 2008, pp. 47–51). Furthermore, the Plan does not include any reference to 'civic participation' of women. Additionally, although setting women quotes for political nominations is a strategy that is often proposed by the women NGOs in order to increase women's participation in local and general elections as nominees, it is not incorporated in the Gender Equality Action Plan, but only mentioned with an indication that there are different views on the quota practice in Turkey (KSGM, 2008, p. 52, see also KSGM, 2009, pp. 26–28). In fact, the perspectives of the public authorities on the women quotes imply that even in relation to this conventional form of participation there are no decisive agenda and related strategies. Thus, the Head of the Grand National Assembly Commission for Equal Opportunity for Women and Men indicates that the real problem in relation to the gender inequality in Turkey is insufficient implementation that has been at issue despite almost 'perfect' legal arrangements.[5] Restricted political participation of women is also stressed by the interviewee as one of the weakest points of the Turkish political landscape. She expresses that the existence of women in local politics was especially restricted due to the high expectations from women who are willing to participate such as being well educated and having a decent family life. Furthermore in her account, in order to promote women's political participation, women quotas in local and national politics should only be implemented as an initial step. In the long run, she indicates, this strategy should be abandoned since women should not be regarded as being in need of such a favour.

Being inactive carries the risk of being ignored during policy-making processes. So women's participation is important to better communicate the preferences and needs of women with public officials (Burns et al., 2001, p. 6). Women's empowerment in participatory behaviour is important not only due to its impact upon policy but also for their recognition as full members of the community (Burns et al., 2001, p. 6). As Tsutsui and Wotipka (2004) mention, considering all segments of society (in equal access of participatory rights and the discussed gender gap in relation to civic/political participation), there could be a transmission effect of participatory behaviour from parents to younger generations.

Alongside the dominant public perspective that is based on an identification of women participation with representation in the parliamentary and local decision-making processes, there are also NGOs sharing this common ground. In the words of an NGO representative:[6] 'In terms of citizenship women's rights have a crucial importance. I wonder that the women in our country are not represented in the parliament on an equal basis. I do not want to be a citizen of a country which is ruled almost only by men.'

Furthermore, two main different NGO positions can be identified in relation to the restricted participation of women in politics in Turkey. The first one identifies the issue with reference to the indifference of women against politics and the underlying reasons of widespread indifference. In parallel with this, the representative of a women's organization points out that fear is the most prominent reason behind women's restricted political engagement.[7] It is also expressed by the interviewee that the foundation in which she works does not prefer to be involved in politics, since its target group is mainly women who are living in poor neighbourhoods and who are mostly housewives having no chance of being active in social life. She describes the main priority of the foundation as to encourage women for gaining self-confidence and economic independence and to provide them opportunities for facilitating their involvement in social life in a more active manner, rather than being involved in political activities. Similarly, a representative from another organization emphasizes that their association is an 'apolitical' one and states that 'we do not have a political approach, in no wise. What is important for us is true implementation of policies related to women'.[8] The second position regards that the gender inequality in terms of political representation should not be conceived as a matter of political indifference on the part of the women. What is at issue is their political exclusion, rather than apathy (KADER, 2006, p. 19).

Furthermore, as it is also the case for both youth NGOs included in the study, there are also women's organizations that perceive political involvement as 'risky' and that mostly abstain from being associated with politics. However, in an accelerating manner in recent years, women's organizations have organized important campaigns on different issues related to women. One of the most prominent is the campaign to politicize the widespread violence against women and the murders, which have started to be widely referred to as 'women murders' and which have claimed that murders of women by men on the grounds of issues such as 'morality', 'honour', and 'jealousy' are not simply murders and they should not be handled simply as such.

Youth

Youth is a category about which a variety of expectations have been framed in different manners in Turkey. Although the age of youth is presented differently in some research and documents in Turkey, the general view is that it is between the ages 12 and 24. According to the Turkish Civil Law (2001), 'Adulthood starts as one finishes the age of eighteen.' According to the Regulations on Youth Centres (2003), individuals should be between the ages of 12 and 24 for the membership to the youth centres, and membership registry can be made, upon request, if the age is no younger than 7 and older than 26. According to the Turkish Civil Law and the Law of Associations (after 2004) every legal and natural person having the capacity to act holds the right to become a member of and establish associations. Also, young people finishing 15 may establish children associations or become members of already established ones. This shows that there is an overlap in age ranges of childhood and youth in Turkey.

As indicated by Kurtaran *et al.* (2008, p. 7) there has been a tendency to conceptualize youth in an instrumental manner, i.e. by assigning certain goals to it as in the case of the widespread phrases such as the 'guarantee of our future'. Although there have been different sorts of such identifications depending on the historical context, the main expectations seem to be framed with reference to the conservative/progressive distinction during the last decade. The first side of the distinction was illustrated by the prime minister, who in one of his public speeches identified one of the goals of the government as 'to raise a faithful generation'.[9] On the other hand, from an oppositional perspective a representative of an NGO, which determines its main target group as the youth, mentions that the organization wishes the young people who engage in their activities to be 'secular, inquisitorial, curious and critical individuals'.[10] She indicates that although the association has no specific programme or project in order to promote young people's participation and engagement, it encourages them to be sensitive in terms of different problems of the country. The main instruments she mentions are the seminars and trainings about different issues and fields that the association organizes for them. She also indicates that they discontinue a scholarship if a scholarship holder does not participate in more than half of the activities the association organizes.

An interviewed member of the Grand National Assembly Commission for National Education, Culture, and Sport from the main oppositional party indicates that there are no peculiar programmes or guidelines that specifically target the civic and political participation of youth in Turkey.[11] A representative of an organization, the aim of which is depicted as working for the active participation of youth in the youth-related decision-making and implementation processes in their own local contexts, indicates that the organization works together with public institutions on the basis of partnership rather than opposition.[12] On the other hand, a recent study (Sener, 2012a) showed that young people associate poverty and unemployment with second-class citizenship and they also refer to cultural discrimination and negative prejudice as important impediments before one's being a full citizen. In the second phase of the same research Ataman *et al.* (2012) show that alongside nationality and rights and obligations, young people tend to refer to social inequalities and income levels in relation to citizenship. This can be revealed from the two basic contexts that young people chose to express their ideas under the headings of unemployment and discrimination. In another study, Sener (2012b) found that even the university students have limited engagement in civic activities where they also have little knowledge about the civic institutions, activities, and projects relating to youth work.

Even though Turkey is a member of the Council of Europe (CoE) and the European Commission, the Revised European Charter for Youth Participation in Local and Regional Life is not being implemented well enough, nor is it a part of the agenda for the local authorities. Youth participation is not one of the key objectives for the youth policy. Furthermore, although there are some ad hoc policies especially to integrate girls into the education system, inequality between young men and women is still an important issue. To be in a rural area or in a smaller city also prevents young people to access many opportunities compared to their peers. Unfortunately, local authorities have limited vision to improve this fact. Accommodation is another important issue for young people. Many young people have to live in another city for their studies and it is not so easy for them to meet their accommodation needs as they desire. Prime Ministry Credit and Dormitories Institution has dormitories for students all around Turkey, however, their capacity is not sufficient to address all students. The regulations for the dormitories are quite strict, highly protective, and not equal at all. For instance, male students have to be in the dormitory at 10:00 pm at the latest, and female students have to be at the dormitory not later than 9:00 pm. Another important point is that these services are provided only for students but not for all young people. Besides accommodation, transportation is another important issue which plays a role in facilitating young people's involvement in the social life. Unfortunately, the subsidies for transportation are very limited. They are only valid for students within their residing town which means that the state supports only students while they are travelling to their schools. Young people who are not in the education system cannot benefit from any support for transportation. The support for young people to get together and have an associated life is very limited. The regulations are not easing the process at all and the awareness about associated life is not sufficient enough. In general, supporting measures are quite limited and not very well known. Consequently, we can say that the youth participation and civic engagement are crucial issues for the youth policy development in Turkey.

Concluding Remarks

The assumption underpinning the analysis presented here is that policy discourse provides a useful indication of key priorities in relation to women and young people's political participation. The analysis reveals the different approaches adopted by policy-makers and NGOs to enhance active citizenship, civic engagement, and political participation. In this respect, this paper makes a contribution to current debates about the position of civic and political participation in Europe.

The first conclusion of this analysis is that there are different approaches to promote women's and youth's participation. This is clearly reflected in the context of the documents analysed here. The elite interviews further support this conclusion. Beginning with youth as a category, these differences stem from the debate on how to conceptualize this particular group. Most commonly, youth is defined as a period in human life, as the transition from childhood to adulthood, and is reduced to a specific age group (Oktay et al., 2010). Another common approach sees youth as the 'most dynamic' stage of life; this group is also seen as the key to *guarantee of the future* and sustainable economic growth. However, even with the changes that effect whole generations, it is not possible to speak of a unitary youth independent of social status. Young people from different social strata experience important social changes in different ways. And yet, it could be argued that in societies which undergo rapid changes, historical and social processes have a great effect on the lives of youth.

In Turkey, there are three types of legal regulations concerning the rights of youth. First, there are laws that are directly about young people, such as Article 59 of the Constitution. The second type consists of laws that do not target youth directly, but nevertheless concern sections of society that are predominantly young. A good example of this kind of regulation is the Disciplinary Code of the Higher Education Credit and Dormitories Institution (Yurt-Kur). The code concerns students, but since the overwhelming majority of university students in Turkey are young people, the main addressee of the law is actually youth. The third type consists of legal regulations that target youths as part of a separate issue, such as employment. Taking the needs of youth in Turkey as the point of departure, the regulations that fall under these three categories need to be revised, improved in content, and in some cases annulled or fully rewritten. Otherwise the gap between increasingly differentiating needs and available services will continue to widen. A regulation that may bridge this gap between young people's needs and the capacities of different institutions that provide services to youth could be a general youth legislation designed as the point of reference for all other laws and regulations that include provisions on youth. Specifying the fundamental duties and responsibilities of the state towards youth in this manner will not only define the rights of youth clearly, but also bring about the extension of these rights into all areas of social life to the benefit of young people. Such a fundamental law could potentially act as a model for future legal regulations developed in favour of other sections of society with different needs. Research (Sherrod, 2007; Skocpol & Fiorina, 1997) indicates that young people associate poverty and unemployment with second-class citizenship and they also refer to cultural discrimination and negative prejudice as important impediments before one's being a full citizen. Furthermore, they claim that they do not have enough information about their rights and obligations as citizens. In general, the perception of participants is firstly related to the duties to be fulfilled as a citizen such as paying taxes and doing military service.

There is not a well-developed mechanism for assessing the needs of young people. The needs are defined quite centrally in line with the general policy approaches not necessarily supported by scientific research and evidence. An evidence-based approach has not developed at all; as a result it is difficult to measure the impact brought about by policy changes. Statistical studies remain quite limited and tangential to the policy process. Only data for youth employment/unemployment rates is constantly collected, however, the studies even for employment fail to address deeper structural issues in relation to youths' fundamental needs.

The youth participation approach should be examined in two dimensions. The first dimension is about the level of youth participation within policy-making processes, which is absent. There is no system for allowing young people to express their ideas and perceptions about the policies targeting them. The second dimension about the policies is how much they reinforce or promote youth participation. Unfortunately, youth-related policies do not aim at developing and promoting youth participation. According to the figures of the Department of Associations, in 2010 there were about 581 youth NGOs in Turkey out of about 89,000 in total. Considering the fact that almost 40% of the population is under 30, this figure represents an important issue. Current policies and regulations do not ease or facilitate the process for youth participation through associated life and NGOs.

In relation to women's participation the dominant perspective of public bodies, as reflected in the documents examined here, can be defined as a narrow approach to 'women's empowerment in participatory behaviour' that is mainly 'representation-centred'. NGO approaches tend to focus on two key issues: (1) restricted participation of women in politics and perceived indifference towards politics and (2) representation and the 'political exclusion of women' from formal structures. It is also important to take into account the intersection of the categories of youth and women, which constitutes the sub-category of young women whose civic and political participation might be regarded as being considerably restricted. In an illustrative study on 'house girls',[13] young women fitting into this category are seen to have limited participation in political, economic, and public life due to the traditional gender roles and family structure (Çelik & Lüküslü, 2012, p. 28).

Finally, existing literature on political participation in Turkey coming from the field of political science has mostly focused on the relation between political participation and electoral behaviour, electoral volatility and democratic consolidation (see, for instance, Kalaycıoglu & Turan, 1981; Ozbudun, 1976). There are studies examining the dynamics of civic and/or political participation behaviour of particular groups (see, for instance, Enneli, 2011; Lüküslü, 2008), but the perspectives of public authorities and NGOs is a clear gap in the current literature.

The analysis presented here suggests a need to increase the visibility in key policy areas in relationship to the political and civic participation of youth and women. The policies on women's participation focused on gender discrimination and equal opportunities. These discourses, therefore, have a significant impact on individuals' access to rights and potentially on the way they see themselves as members of a political community. The findings of the PIDOP project have important implications for policy-makers and civil society actors.[14] Among them, the need for the policy-makers' consideration of the fact that policies are influencing the ways in which citizens interact with both state and non-state actors is an essential one. On the other hand, it is essential to take into account that gender, culture, ethnicity, religion, and age interact with one another in citizens' identifications and behaviours in the policy discourse. As mentioned earlier in this paper, the lack of measures to evaluate the participation levels of women and young people is important to develop better understanding and the recognition of these groups. Consequently, follow-up studies are needed to develop working plans.

Acknowledgements

This research was supported by a grant received from the European Commission seventh Framework Programme, FP7-SSH-2007-1, Grant Agreement no: 225282, Processes Influencing Democratic Ownership and Participation (PIDOP) awarded to the University of Surrey (UK), University of Liège (Belgium), Masaryk University (Czech Republic), University of Jena (Germany), University of Bologna (Italy), University of Porto (Portugal), Örebro University (Sweden), Ankara University (Turkey), and Queen's University Belfast (UK).

The work for this project was conducted as part of a team. The author would like to thank to her team members, namely Prof Figen Cok and and Sumercan Bozkurt, for their great contributions to this paper as well as their contributions throughout the project.

Notes

1. During the review process of this paper, a civil movement had begun in Turkey. The occupation of Taksim Gezi Park in İstanbul began on 28 May 2013. Following the police raid in the park area on 30 May, the occupation continued, and thousands of people gathered to resist the government's plans (to build a shopping centre and destroy the green area). It soon became one of the largest mobilizations for years, with various different participants (from radical activists to NGOs, etc.), resembling the worldwide Occupy movement. On 31 May, street clashes started from 5:00 am in İstanbul. The resistance grew wider, while the police fired an incredible amount of tear gas bombs. An environmental protest in Istanbul which then became an anti-government move is still continuing throughout the country.
2. Although the research realized by the Ankara team within the scope of the PIDOP Project encompassed two additional groups, i.e. Roma people and the Turkish Resettlers from Bulgaria under the category of minority/immigrant, they are not included in this article for three reasons. First is the fact that there are no public and NGO documents that are directly related to the civic and political participations of these groups. Second, the dynamics of immigration as well as the characteristics of immigrant populations imply important differences compared to the European cases which are included in the project. And finally, there is an ambiguity concerning the term 'minority' in Turkey. Since the foundation of the Turkish Republic, the only protection for minorities has been that set out in the 1923 Treaty of Lausanne. In the Treaty only the non-Muslim population (Armenians, Jews, and Christians with Greek origin) were defined as minority (Minority Rights Group International, 2007). There is also no legislative framework for other ethnic or religious groups in Turkey, either directly through laws granting minority rights or indirectly through an anti-discrimination law (Minority Rights Group International, 2007).
3. For the mentioned database see http://www.stgm.org.tr/en/stoveritabani.
4. Like its European counterparts, the Turkish National Agency is an organization responsible for organizing and coordinating the EU-based education and youth programmes in Turkey.
5. Interview made by the authors on 7 April 2010.
6. Interview made by the authors with the Head of Modern Women and Youth Foundation on 3 May 2010.
7. Interview made by the authors with the Head of Modern Women and Youth Foundation on 3 May 2010.
8. Interview made by the authors with the Head of Association of Business and Professional Women on 10 April 2010.
9. See the related news: 'We will raise a faithful generation.' Available at http://www.hurriyet.com.tr/gundem/19825231.asp, February 2, 2012 (accessed on 18 September 2012).
10. Interview made by the authors with a representative of Association for Support of Modern Life on 5 May 2010.
11. Interview made by the authors on 7 April 2010.
12. Interview made by the authors with a representative of Youth Association for Habitat (Youth for Habitat) on 4 April 2010.
13. The 'house girl' (*Ev kızı* in Turkish) refers to the young woman who is neither part of the formal education system nor the labour market (Çelik & Lüküslü, 2012, p. 29). This category is characterized with those who 'do not get married immediately after leaving school (as it was the case traditionally) and do not get the "status" of a married woman and house wife' (Çelik & Lüküslü, 2012, p. 29).
14. A detailed report of the policy recommendations of the PIDOP Project can be found at the links below: http://www.fahs.surrey.ac.uk/pidop/documents/PIDOP%20Policy%20Recommendations.pdf, http://www.fahs.surrey.ac.uk/pidop/documents/Briefings/PIDOP%20Policy%20Briefing%20Paper%20No.%201.pdf.

References

Ataman, A., Cof, F. & Sener, T. (2012) Understanding civic engagement among young Roma and young Turkish people in Turkey, *Human Affairs*, 22(3), pp. 419–433.

Ayata, A. & Tütüncü, F. (2008) Party politics of the AKP (2002–2007) and the predicaments of women at the intersection of the Westernist, Islamist and Feminist discourses in Turkey, *British Journal of Middle Eastern Studies*, 35(3), pp. 363–384.

Barrett, M. (2011) Opening plenary paper presented at the Bologna PIDOP conference, "Engaged Citizens? Political Participation and Civic Engagement Among Youth, Women, Minorities and Migrants", University of Bologna, Bologna, Italy, 11–12 May.

Berry, J. (1997) Technology, participation, and community, *American Planning Association. Journal of the American Planning Association*, 63(2), pp. 287–289.

Burns, N., Lehman Schlozman, K. & Verba, S. (2001) *The Private Roots of Public Action* (Cambridge, MA: Harvard University Press).

Çelik, K. & Lüküslü, D. (2012) Spotlighting a silent category of young females: The life experiences of 'house girls' in Turkey, *Youth and Society*, 44(1), pp. 28–48.

Ekman, J. & Amnå, E. (2012) Political participation and civic engagement: Towards a new typology, *Human Affairs*, 22(3), pp. 283–300.

Enneli, P. (2011) The Turkish young people as active citizens: Equal participation or social exclusion? in: R. Ö. Dönmez & P. Enneli (Eds) *Societal Peace and Ideal Citizenship for Turkey*, pp. 257–280 (Lanham, MD: Lexington Books).

KADER [Kadın Adayları Destekleme Derneği, Association for the Support of Women Candidates] (2006) *Cinsiyet Eşitliği Yolunda Yerel Politikalar Raporu* [Report on the Local Politics on the Road to Gender Equality] (Ankara: KADER).

Kalaycioglu, E. & Turan, I. (1981) Measuring political participation: A cross cultural application, *Comparative Political Studies*, 14(1), pp. 123–135.

KSGM [Kadının Statusu Genel Mudurlugu, General Directorate on the Status of Women] (2008) *National Action Plan, Gender Equality: 2008–2013* (Ankara: The Republic of Turkey Prime Ministry, General Directorate on the Status of Women).

KSGM [Kadının Statusu Genel Mudurlugu, General Directorate on the Status of Women] (2009) *Turkiye'de Kadının Durumu* [State of Woman in Turkey] (Ankara: The Republic of Turkey Prime Ministry, General Directorate on the Status of Women).

Kurtaran, Y., Nemutlu, G. & Yentürk, N. (2008) About, for, and together with youth: A summary of 'youth work and policy in Turkey', in: N. Yentürk, Y. Kurtaran & G. Nemutlu (Eds) *Youth Work and Policy in Turkey*, pp. 6–20. Research Paper, no.3 (Istanbul Bilgi University Youth Study Unit).

Lüküslü, D. (2008) Günümüz Türkiye Gençliği: Ne Kayıp Bir Kuşak Ne de Ülkenin Aydınlık Geleceği, in: N. Yentürk, Y. Kurtaran & G. Nemutlu (Eds) *Türkiye'de Gençlik Çalışması ve Politikaları*, pp. 287–297 (İstanbul: İstanbul Bilgi Üniversitesi Yayınları).

Minority Rights Group International (2007) *A Quest for Equality: Minorities in Turkey*, Report (London: Minority Rights Group International).

Oktay, F., Şentuna, M., Cenk, M., Görbil, V. & Şener, T. (2010) Youth policy in Turkey, in: E. Bornemark & V. Görbil (Eds) *Introduction to Youth Policy: Swedish and Turkish Perspectives*, pp. 12–19 (Sweden: Ungdomsstyrelsen).

Ozbudun, E. (1976) *Social Change and Political Participation in Turkey* (Princeton, NJ: Princeton University Press).

Pachi, D. & Barrett, M. (2012) Perceived effectiveness of conventional, non-conventional and civic forms of participation among minority and majority youth, *Human Affairs*, 22(3), pp. 345–359.

Seckinelgin, H. (2006) Civil society between the state and society: Turkish women with Muslim headscarves, *Critical Social Policy*, 26(4), pp. 748–769.

Sener, T. (2012a) The Effects of Experiences in Participation among Turkish Youth. 15th European Conference on Developmental Psychology, Bologna, Medimond, pp. 435–440.

Sener, T. (2012b) Civic engagement of future teachers, *Procedia: Technology*, 1(1), pp. 4–7.

Sherrod, L. (2007) Civic engagement as an expression of positive youth development, in: K. Rainer, R. Silbereisenve & M. Lerner (Eds) *Approaches to Positive Youth Development*, pp. 59–74 (London: Sage Publications).

Skocpol, T. & Fiorina, M. P. (1997) *Civic Engagement in American Society*, pp. 1–27 (Washington DC: Brookings Institution Press).

TSI [Turkish Statistical Institute] (2012) *Youth in Statistics, 2011* (Ankara: Turkish Statistical Institute Printing Division).

Tsutsui, K. & Wotipka, C. (2004) Global civil society and the international human rights movement: Citizen participation in human rights international nongovernmental organizations, *Social Forces*, 83(2), pp. 587–620.

Verba, S., Schlozman, K. L. & Brady, H. E. (1995) *Voice and Equality: Civic Voluntarism in American Politics* (Cambridge, MA: Harvard University Press).

Zani, B. & Barrett, M. (2012) Introduction: Engaged citizens? Political participation and social engagement among youth, women, minorities, and migrants, *Human Affairs*, 22(3), pp. 273–282.

Zukin, C., Keeter, S., Andolina, M., Jenkins, K. & Delli Carpini, M. X. (2006) *A New Engagement, Political Participation, Civic Life, and the Changing American Citizen* (New York: Oxford University Press).

On Active Citizenship: Discourses and Language about Youth and Migrants in Italy

PAOLA VILLANO* & ALBERTO BERTOCCHI**

*Department of Education, School of Psychology and Education, University of Bologna, Bologna, Italy;
**Independent Psychologist, Bologna, Italy

ABSTRACT *The civic and political participation of young people and especially young migrants, who have limited rights of citizenship, is still a significant problem in Italy. Young people struggle to find opportunities and feel excluded from politics: the political agenda tends to see them more as a problem than as a resource. In this article, we illustrate the results of research to understand the dynamics of political and civic participation of young people and what the policy does in their favour. A content analysis of a corpus of European and Italian legislation, policy and planning documents has been undertaken. We also conducted six in-depth interviews with politicians and representatives of Italian nongovernmental organizations in order to investigate (a) policy priorities and institutional points of view, (b) consistency between these priorities and European programmes, and (c) European Union support for the policy actions and projects promoted in Italy about youth. The results showed a general difficulty for young people to 'engage' and be engaged in civic and political activities. There is also a gap between the political level and an effective investment which will recognize young people as a real resource.*

Citizenship is frequently invoked as both an instrument and a goal of immigrant integration and is a crucial word in Italy, where migrants born on national soil still do not have rights. In this article, we are interested in studying the issue of the discourse and language of some Italian politicians and nongovernmental organizations (NGOs) on the issues of youth and migration. Through analysis of legislation and interviews with politicians and representatives of the NGOs, this article seeks to understand the dynamics of political and civil participation and also what is being done at the political level for young people and migrants in Italy. In particular, we examined the causes that encourage (or fail to do so) political participation and engagement on the part of youth and migrants, and the role—and the motivations—of young generations in taking an active part in civil society. In fact, as suggested by some studies, in the Italian political agenda youth is still seen as a 'problem' rather than as a resource: consequently, in the face of this legal vacuum and lack of opportunities, young people feel excluded from the policies and decisions affecting them.

Six in-depth interviews were conducted with Italian politicians and representatives of NGOs in order to investigate (a) political priorities and institutional points of view; (b) the coherence between these priorities and European programmes; and (c) European Union support for political actions and projects in Italy. The interviews were analysed using content analysis. The results showed a general lack of motivation for civic and political engagement, due to the deep gap with Europe which is perceived as being too distant. The article is divided into two sections: following an overview of European legislation and especially the Italian laws on youth and young migrants, in the second part we present the content analysis of six interviews and a discussion of results.

Political Participation and Citizenship: Some Theoretical Definitions

The European Commission defines 'citizenship as equal membership in a political community to which rights and duties, participatory practices, benefits and a sense of identity are attached' (European Commission, 2013, p. 14). Some researchers have examined the historical development of the concept of citizenship, and found three elements which appear to be constantly present: 'namely, appurtenance (the feeling of belonging to the politic party), passive citizenship (protection by the polity) and active citizenship (participation in the polity)' (Smirnov-Brkíc et al., 2010, p. 2).

The concept of citizenship is related obviously to political participation: the good citizen, among other things, is he/she who feels invested with civic responsibility and puts to use an active behaviour intended to influence political outcomes in society (Teorell et al., 2007; Theiss-Morse, 1993). Teorell et al. (2007) developed a definition of political participation that takes into account five important dimensions: (1) electoral participation, (2) consumer participation, that is the role of the citizen as a critical consumer (signing petitions or boycotting certain products), (3) party activity, such as being a member of or an activist within a party, (4) protest activity, such as taking part in protests and strikes, and (5) contact activity, which consists in contacting organizations, politicians, or public officials.

This type of participation highlights the manifest forms that characterize it, but there is also another form of political participation that always distinguishes the majority of citizens, that is a latent participation (equally incisive) which refers to 'pre-political' aims (Amnå, 2010). Such actions include, for example, not going to vote, writing a letter of protest to the newspapers, or collecting waste, any of which may have an important meaning for political activities. There is also another important dimension: attention to and interest in political and social issues (social involvement), which also includes awareness of being a member of a society (Martin & van Deth, 2007). These actions go under the name of civil participation which is manifest in behaviours that are defined as latent in relation to specific policy actions on the part of parliamentarians. The notion, therefore, of latent political participation is a theoretical innovation because it helps us to understand the confusion generated in part by the decline of manifest political participation (voter turnout), but at the same time an increase of civic interest and latent actions (Ekman &

Amnå, 2009; Zani *et al.*, 2011). In this article, we focus on this latent dimension of participation, closely linked to the dimension of citizenship.

Fieldwork Context

June 2011 marks the beginning of a new way of doing politics and above all of taking part in politics in Italy. The ratification of four popular referenda[1] represents an example of bottom-up politics. Citizen-centred committees were central to this success. Organized on the basis of social networks, they informed and gave voice to young citizens, who in the process (re)discovered an interest in public affairs. In other words, this is an example of open and deliberative policy-making. Media discourse around increased participation focused on the role of young people, who are represented as the true actors and protagonists of civic and political participation.

As some studies have shown (Cuconato *et al.*, 2012; Mesa, 2010), in Italy there is a large gap between 'the rhetoric of the institutional principles and the real praxis of the Italian youth policies, which very often continues to be limited to cultural practices' (Cuconato *et al.*, 2012, p. 94), neglecting the real need for the political engagement of the young. Youth show low levels of trust in existing decision-making structures and lack interest in traditional forms of political participation, while studies show an increase in so-called 'non-parliamentary forms' of participation and civic participation (Ekman & Amnå, 2009; Zani *et al.*, 2011). In general, youth are more likely to experience indifference and a sense of disaffection towards traditional forms of politics. In some cases, they turn to alternative forms of political participation, for example, websites or social networks (Loncle *et al.*, 2012), as well as spontaneous informal forms of association where young people feel more involved in decision-making processes. According to Sciolla (2004), the apathy expressed towards politics and politicians by young Italians reflects an underlying indifference and mistrust having the potential to endanger the very roots of democratic life.

The evidence reported in these studies is worrying, particularly in the context of an ageing of the population. From a socio-demographic perspective, the EU will be able to slow down the shift in the population structure only through immigration. According to Eurostat data,[2] young people (16–26 years of age) make up 13.5% of the total EU population. In Italy the demographic crisis is even more acute, whereby youth only make up 11.3% of the total Italian population. Looking at the decade 2002–2011, while the total population of Europe and Italy has increased, the youth population for the range considered has decreased. Italy also turns out to be the country with the highest mean age (44.6 years), well above the European average (40.9 years).

In Italy citizenship is traditionally based on communitarian values. This has important repercussions for the position of migrants and their access to citizenship rights. Notably, this issue has yet to find a place on the political agenda. The exclusion of migrants from citizenship rights is not only due to the prevailing norm of *ius sanguinis* (the principle that a person's nationality at birth is the same as that of his/her natural parents), but more significantly because of the lack of political engagement with the issue. State institutions and political actors have adopted a utilitarian approach to the issue, whereby it only appears on the policy agenda for strategic and opportunistic reasons, i.e. in the case of administrative elections.

But when the new centre-left government was sworn into office, things changed. On 28 April 2013 in fact, Cecile Kyenge Kashetu, of Congolese origin, was appointed Minister for International Cooperation and Integration. This might give some hope of launching appropriate reforms concerning the issues of integration of young migrants. In particular, the new Minister began her tenure by promoting a bill on the recognition of citizenship to migrant children born to parents who legally resided in Italy for at least five years, and the possibility to request it even for those not born, but raised in Italy.

The Minister's programme provides some points whose implementation could be an important step in terms of integration, equal opportunities and citizenship of migrants, and the cancellation of the current law on immigration (Bossi-Fini Law no. 189) put in place in 2002 by a centre-right government. These include introducing *ius soli* (the right to nationality based on place of birth) and the institution of detention, repealing the criminalization of illegal immigration, revising the requirements for family reunification in order to give certainty to the right to family unity, and granting political rights to foreigners with permanent residence.

In dealing with the issue of migration and citizenship, Italy is only now being faced with questions relating to 'second generations'. In this regard, we need to draw attention to a 20-year-old law (Law n. 91, 5 February 1992, *Nuove norme sulla cittadinanza* [New rules on citizenship]), considered to be one of the most restrictive in Europe. This policy is important in relation to the analysis presented here in as far as it regulates the right to citizenship. In Italy, the *ius sanguinis* principle rules the acquisition of citizenship. By contrast, in Germany, the state has adapted to be more inclusive of 'second generation migrants'. After 2000 if a child is born on German soil to foreign parents he/she can have German nationality if one parent has had a permanent permit of stay for at least three years and has been a resident for at least eight.

In Italy, there are much stricter qualifying rules for naturalization. In order to have the right to request citizenship, a foreign national must show he/she has had uninterrupted and regular residence for ten years, showing he/she earns a declared income that guarantees self-sufficiency of around €8.000 per year, €11.000 with a spouse to care for, plus €516 for each child, if he/she has any. The child of foreign nationals born in Italy can apply for citizenship on his/her 18th birthday.

This rather laborious and complex procedure and the diverse policies managing migration that have been successively implemented since 1998 have certainly not helped the civic and political participation of migrants in Italy (Kosic, 2007). According to Colombo (2012), while the state's interest in controlling external borders complies with a legitimate policy issued by the EU, the group of migrants, in particular illegal migrants, has often been criminalized (also by the mass media), and this has led to their progressive stigmatization and marginalization from society, with an inevitable and progressive distancing from political life. Indeed, young migrants, unlike their Italian peers, cannot vote or register for public elections.

The Rete G2—Second Generations (The Network G2), an important national, non-partisan organization founded by the children of migrants and refugees born and/or raised in Italy, summarizes the major difficulties of the second generation in Italy resulting from the current legislation (http://www.secondegenerazioni.it/):

- The obligation to renew the residence permit with all the problems associated with delays and red tape and the consequent complications for entering school.

- The difficulty in travelling and the consequent limitations of the residence permit.
- Those born in Italy can apply for citizenship at the age of 18 but must have lived continuously on the Italian territory and they must be able to prove it.
- Obstacles at school: According to a rule by the ex-Minister of Education Gelmini, no class can exceed a certain percentage of foreign students. Children whose mother tongue is Italian, therefore, may not be able to attend school in their neighbourhood because they are considered foreigners. College students cannot participate in study periods abroad with Italian or European exchange projects such as Erasmus.
- If a child was not born in Italy and only arrived here at a young age, he/she cannot apply for citizenship at the age of 18.
- The second generation cannot vote.

It is evident then that political participation of foreign nationals, supported both at the national and local levels, ends up being limited to a merely consultative function, performed by means of the creation of forums and committees, elected bodies that represent, within the above limits, an opportunity for representation of the different communities in dialogue with local government. Some municipalities have also introduced in their statutes the position of adjunct councillor who, elected by the foreign nationals, flanks the municipal councillors in their representative function.

Aims and Method

In this article, we try to understand what role young people and young migrants play in political and civil participation in Italy, through the 'discourses' of politicians and representatives of NGOs who promote projects for young people and young migrants. The focus lies on the opportunities and constraints upon political participation (active and latent) of marginal groups in Italy. Thus, in addition to analysing official legal documents, we conducted interviews with politicians and NGOs in order to understand and discuss their views on civic and political participation of youth and migrants.

The importance of analysing the discourse of both politicians and NGOs lies in the fact that it highlights 'political' priorities. The political debate, for example, presupposes a series of distinct elements, such as the role of the democratic institutions in a given society, the functions, the tasks and the conceptions of and about the parliamentarians, and the relations of political institutions with various social institutions, the media, and citizens.

When we speak of citizenship and nationality, we reflect on some precise frames that are constructed and conditioned by the wider political context. For example, narratives around citizenship in Italy take on a different shape from other European countries, regardless of whether the focus is on young people or migrants. As a consequence, analysing discourse not only allows us to identify key themes; it also highlights the parameters of the debate (Entman, 1993). As Bee and Scartezzini (2009) have outlined, the political system and its discursive practices take on a crucial role in the development of the individuals' political identity, and this is an important aspect that cannot be overlooked in psychosocial research. What transpires is that the condition of being a citizen in a complex reality cannot be simply understood via institutional dynamics. In order to unpack the different dimensions of citizenship we need to reconstruct those discursive threads that underlie such a fluid concept. This is all the more important as its core principles help to define the membership of the community.

Active Citizenship of Young People and Migrants: The Italian Legislative Framework

This section offers an overview of the main laws concerning the promotion and the support for participative processes, as well as the entitlement to and the exercise of citizenship for young people. We explore both the normative aspects of the legislation as well as the main 'instruments' of participation available and used in national and regional policies. The documents, identified using Italian institutional websites,[3] allowed us to gather the information needed in order to trace the policy process and identify key institutional actors in the planning and implementation stages. Both regional and national policies are examined to allow for a more fine-grained understanding of the assumptions underpinning the policy agenda targeting young people and migrants.

The analysis of the documentation focused on the following aspects: (1) citizenship and rights, participation and equal opportunities; (2) instruments and processes foreseen for the participation and removal of the obstacles (committees, panels, action plans, funding, and programme agreements); and (3) fields of intervention (policies, culture, social, volunteering, and education). Overall, we examined 32 national and regional documents, including the Italian constitution, 7 national policies and 1 regional policy, and a range of planning documents.

The National Legislative Framework

The first important national references that concern young people appear in the Constitution. In particular, in Section 31, it is stated that the Republic 'Protects maternity, infancy and youth, fostering the provisions necessary for that purpose.' This article frames the relationship between young people and the state that is defined by a specific understanding of the role of the family within society. Youth are seen less as active citizens and more as a protected category. That said, references to participative processes and equal opportunities are already present in the Italian Constitution, although they are limited by the hierarchical and paternalistic nature of its normative foundations.

The principles of equality are also reiterated on a number of occasions: 'All the citizens have equal social dignity and are equal before the law, without differences between gender, race, language, religion, political views, personal and social conditions' (Section 3 of the Constitution of the Italian Republic). In the same article it is also stated that:

> ... it is the task of the Republic to remove the obstacles of an economic and social kind that, de facto by curbing freedom and equality among citizens, prevent the full development of the person and the effective participation of all the workers in the political, economic and social organization of the country. (art. 3 of Italian Constitution)

These defining principles were included to deal specifically with the fields of education, employment, and political participation, stating in various sections (Sections 3, 29, 37, 51, 117) the guarantee of the key socio-economic rights such as education, work, and political organization. These are principles that are applied to all citizens regardless of gender, race, language, political opinions, and personal and social status.

In the field of youth policies, the task of translating these constitutional principles into laws is transferred to the Regions (Section 117 of the Constitution). There are no national laws targeting specifically youth. The organizational history of the Youth Ministry highlights some of the shortcomings of the Italian approach. In 2006, the Ministry for Youth Policies and Sports Activities (POGAS) was set up, thus giving Italy, on a par with most of the other European countries, a department for youth policies. POGAS brought together the competencies relating to youth issues with those for sport. It was replaced in 2008 by the Ministry for Youth, only preserving the competences relating to youth policies. In particular, the Ministry deals with the following tasks:

- The juridical and administrative requirements and the execution of the actions concerning the performance of the functions on the subject of youth, with particular reference to the affirmation of the rights of young people to freedom of speech, also in the forms of associations, their needs, and interests, and the right to take part in public life.
- The promotion of the right of young people to a home, to skills, and technological innovation, to support for work and youth entrepreneurship.
- The promotion of and support for the creative activities and the cultural initiatives of young people and initiatives concerning leisure time, cultural, and educational trips.
- Support to young people's access to projects, plans, and international and community funding. (http://www.gioventu.gov.it).

This important change in the Italian legal scenario has had a positive impact on young people, who have started to be recognized as social subjects and as the target of services and projects stemming from the national and local administrations. The creation of a dedicated Ministry focusing on young people certainly marks an important turning point for encouraging a deeper involvement and an active participation of local youth associations (Mesa, 2010). This change has also contributed to the creation of new professional profiles and the establishment of the first educational and youth labour cooperatives, which have played an extremely active role over recent years.

Within this administrative/organizational framework, it is up to the Regions to pass laws addressed to promoting active citizenship among the young people. This means that there is large variation in the quality and scope of the policies. An example is the Emilia Romagna region's Regional Law no. 14 (28 July 2008) on 'Norms on the subject of policies for the young generations.' The policy's target is children, adolescents, and youth with a view to providing continuity and coherence to local policies and to guaranteeing full personal development to young people, irrespective of ethnicity, citizenship, and residence. This piece of legislation seeks to safeguard the physical, mental, and social health and well-being of young generations. It also seeks to promote equal opportunities for youth to ensure personal growth and fulfilment. It places high value on diversity and equality; the participation of young generations in civil and social life; and the promotion of active citizenship and intergenerational, intercultural, and inter-religious dialogue to support the cohesion and the growth of the community. Finally, it supports education for peace and social solidarity, the sustainability of the urban environment, the right of young people to be informed, educated, and trained and to play, leisure time, culture, art and sport, and the right to health.

In particular, in regard to active citizenship, the law promotes mobility and European citizenship, in line with European programmes; support for various forms of youth association aiming at the exercise of activities dedicated to young people; and support for the involvement of young people in the decision-making process by means of the practices of e-democracy. These provisions allow the region to support associations and organizations working to promote volunteering and other services directly benefiting youth groups. Local authorities are the main delivery mechanism for these policies, particularly in relation to political participation and representation in decision-making processes.

Instruments and Enforcement: Unpacking the Political Dimension of Policies Targeting Youth and Migrants

The main instrument for enforcing youth policies in Italy is the *Piano Nazionale Giovani* (National Youth Plan) which, benefiting from funding that comes from the national fund for youth policies, defines the strategic plan for each Region in relation to youth policies. The document makes explicit reference to promoting participation, active citizenship, and volunteering. It implicitly recognizes and supports associations and other forms of youth organization.

Equally important for promoting participation among young people is the National Civil Service, set up by Law no. 64 (6 March 2001).[4] This is a volunteer service for young people aged between 18 and 28 years, whose aim is to offer an opportunity for social, civic, cultural, and professional training by means of human experience of social solidarity, activities of national and international cooperation, and safeguarding and protection of the national heritage.

Finally, the National Youth Forum recognized by Law no. 311 (30 December 2004) represents another opportunity for exchange and participation. It is a national platform of Italian youth organizations representing around four million young people. It seeks to create a space for debate. A diverse group of youth organizations (political parties, religious associations, student groups, etc.) come together under this umbrella to share and exchange experiences. The Forum performs a consultative and propositional role on the subject of youth policies. It also promotes the civic and political participation of young people by supporting the creation and development of volunteer organizations.

As regards the migrant youth there are a number of laws dealing specifically with citizenship provisions of third-country nationals. It must be said, however, that this body of legislation in mainly concerned with access to and regulation of residence. There are no specific provisions relating to young people or active citizenship. Particularly worthy of attention is Law No. 189 (30 July 2002, amending the legislation on matters of immigration and asylum).

In Brief

From the analysis of the laws, there appears at the national level a change that concerns young people with the inception in 2006 of the first ministry with specific competencies for young people and the creation of a fund to support youth programmes. In this system it is the Regions that become the true policy-makers, bringing the places of governance closer to the young people and the territory.

From a political viewpoint, attention to different forms of active participation of young people, volunteering, associations, and culture has not been very widespread so far. At the national level great importance is given to the active involvement of young people in the

EU's political and civic construction, particularly in response to the difficulties that they are facing in terms of developing a sense of European membership and citizenship.

Unpacking Counter Narratives: Civil Society's Understanding of Citizenship and Participation

The overview of the formal legal framework presented above provides useful insights into official Italian discourse about citizenship and participation, youth, and migrants. It is, however, only a partial picture. This section now turns its attention to the position of civil society organizations and NGOs focusing on young people and migrants. Within the scope of the PIDOP project[5] interviews have been conducted with policy-makers and representatives of civil society organizations. The aim was to understand their position about citizenship and political participation. In-depth interviews provide a useful source of data about foundational norms and operational values of the organization and the individuals working for them. The interviews also allow us to single out the actions that are performed to encourage the involvement and the participation of the target groups.

Six people were interviewed—representatives of the NGOs and policy-makers—who operate at the national and international levels in the fields considered (young people and migrants). The in-depth interviews explore: (1) political priorities and the points of view of the institutions; (2) coherence between the priorities and the directives and/or European programmes (where this is envisaged); and (3) European support for political actions and projects.

Young People

Research looking to understand active citizenship has to take into account both the political and cultural contexts within which it is performed. Context-based research shows how the physical contexts in which people live and interact affect the information they receive and the social meanings they construct (Anderson, 2010). Social forces, that is to say the people we live, work, and socialize with, play a crucial role in determining the choices that are made, including the level of political involvement and the political attitude, as well as the construction of a national and European identity. Unpacking the processes and values that underpin citizenship requires a detailed analysis of the political and psychological dimensions as well as the legal foundations that allow citizens to exercise their rights in a socio-political context. By way of analysis of the interviews we can report and reconstruct a broad picture and a more complex vision of the themes that reflect on citizenship and political and civic participation.

Two questions provide a springboard for our research and interviews: What is done for young people at the political level? What are the forces that feed participation, engagement, and ownership in a democratic context?

The picture that emerges from our interviews brings to mind a patchwork painting, with parts that are complete but still with many 'gaps' that need to be filled in. There are bills and legislative proposals addressing the development and promotion of youth associations (but that then end up stuck in parliamentary commissions and whose outcomes remain unknown). There is also the real possibility for enhancing the quality of political participation of young people by giving those aged 14–29 the possibility to vote in the political primary elections of the Democratic Party (since 2005). However, an increasing awareness has emerged that many young people are oriented towards other forms of participation (perhaps more indirect) thus signalling a rejection of traditional forms of participation and engagement:

> My perception is that if we could measure this condition in respect to the different aspects [of politics], vote, petitions, information, etc., we would note participation data that are not unlike those of other countries. From what I can understand, today a certain part of this discontinuous, occasional and in any case unorganized participation goes via the Internet... (Interviewed Member of Parliament)

'Bottom-up' processes for participation of young people are recognized as one of the significant forces behind change: the activities of networks which, for example, are not part of the establishment, are able to influence important choices (such as the preference for a mayoral candidate). This is an interesting aspect, which takes us back to the concept of membership in a community, closely connected to that of citizenship (McMillan & Chavis, 1986). As has been shown by the psychosocial research in this field, the social interaction thus offers a range of positive resources at both the individual and the collective level, stimulating and motivating collective participation (Claibourne & Martin, 2002; La Due Lake & Huckfeldt, 1998; Putnam, 1993, 1995).

With respect to the European question, one interview with a Member of Parliament highlights the missed opportunities offered by the process of European integration:

> (T)he perception that the opportunities offered by the European Community for the promotion of participation of young people are not fully utilized.

In other words, national programmes for young people follow European directives (e.g. measures supporting youth associations), so there is supposedly no discrepancy between national and European levels. The problem lies in taking advantage of all the opportunities, perhaps not yet fully exploited.

The theme of European citizenship and its meaning clearly emerges from the interviews with political leaders. European integration is promoted (and supported) by the greater mobility of students and workers, by the dynamism of the market. The greater propensity of young people to move, thanks to study programmes (e.g. Erasmus exchanges), allows them to experience different lifestyles, socio-cultural contexts, and political traditions. Yet our interviewee is also cautious, noting an element of decreased enthusiasm for the European project, particularly following the introduction of the Euro. In practice, in the 1990s Europe has had a positive effect because Euro membership:

> has allowed governments to enforce recovery policies that are otherwise impossible and as there was a positive expectation in respect to the European Union the costs have not been paid enthusiastically but they have been put up with. Now with the economic crisis this concept no longer applies; actually it is depressing the positive identification with Europe (as is happening now with the Greek crisis).

The representatives of the NGOs (e.g. Arci—Italian Recreational and Cultural Association and Ucodep—Unity and Cooperation for the Development of Peoples) have a different way of framing the discussion about citizenship. They have a tendency to interpret the concept of youth citizenship according to the projects promoted. Citizenship is understood as 'education in global citizenship' which includes information, sensitization, and mobilization. Civil society thus becomes an actor of change capable of influencing in a positive way political decisions at the local, national, and European levels. All of this must be realized starting from a fundamental field: that of school and training in general.

The projects promoted by the NGOs at the national level are interdependent with the European level, because:

> what is happening in the world has repercussions on our country and territory [...] and here there is the element of risk and the opportunity as citizenship and public opinion experience the processes of transformation following the impetuous globalization of the past twenty years. (F.P. President Ucodep and President of Italian Association of NGOs)

According to the President of the Italian Association of NGOs, in order to promote a democracy that hails the young people as protagonists, it is necessary to create a system of democratic participation in which the civil societies and their representatives can dialogue and impact the decisions of the governments.

The European Commission (2013) has said that there is a need for coherence in development policies and indicated five fundamental areas: aid, trade, security, the fight against poverty, and sustainable development. Understood within this wider political context, a universal right to citizenship becomes key to the exercise of democracy and is manifested in coherent social policies and actions at all levels: 'I would ask Europe to make one of its key words come alive: that is, social cohesion' (F.P. President Ucodep and President of Italian Association of NGOs). This is the specific aim of Arci: to bring together young people by means of participation pathways, with a view to making them responsible and make them active subjects. Youth, including migrants, are 'welcomed in respect to their propositional capacities', so as to allow them to 'demand their rights and be able to aspire to growth'. But in respect to these projects, lack of suitable policies and a cultural drift is denounced:

> When you have a country in which there are cuts in training and culture and which does not invest in research, in universities, in schools, it is evident that we are all getting poorer.

As for the politicians and the representatives of the NGOs, the Italians, and in particular the young people, experience Europe as being far away, mainly due to lack of opportunities to affect decision-making and in terms of their active involvement in participative processes. The interviews manifest a sense of distrust in Europe. The EU and its associated institutions have not been able to exert the necessary authority on the citizens and/or have failed to capture the public's imagination: As the interviewees indicated, 'It's as though the idea of Europe had not taken root deeply' owing to a lack of concrete actions. Europe is still just an idea, without there being a real participation and its recognition by the people.

Migrants

'The right to vote, the right to education, the right to work': This could be the summary slogan that characterizes the discourse on migrants in the words of the NGOs and the politicians.

Looking at the political arena, the interviewees (one MP and one official of the First General Directorate of Immigration, Ministry of Employment and Social Policies) claim that the action plans for migrants aim at several important fields: access to school, health, public services, housing, work, and the knowledge of Italian. The focus of attention is to establish some form of collaboration between formal political institutions on the one hand and migrants' associations or NGOs on the other. This approach seeks to ensure that resources that should foster integration and participation of the migrants are deployed as effectively and efficiently as possible. Indeed, collaboration with the associations that perform activities in favour of the migrants represents an important asset with and on which to work, so as to translate the abstract concept of citizenship into practices of daily life.

According to the MP interviewed for this project, with respect to migrants Italy has a major deficit. There is:

> definitely a conflict that depends on the government's immigration policies and in particular those of the last few years that head in directions that at times clearly clash with the community directives and not only as regards the promotion of participation, that is a subject that has almost vanished, but even as regards the safeguarding of rights.

The interview highlights the privileged position of formal employment as a pathway for migrant integration. In this context, employee protection plays a crucial role, particularly in terms of safeguarding of health, security of the migrant worker, and continuous training so as to be able to be re-employed in the case of redundancy and fair pay. Arguably, it is for this reason that the Ministry has set up the 'Consulta' (Advisory Panel) to address the problems of third-country nationals working on Italian territory. The Consulta offers a table for discussion and negotiations, which foresees the presence of representatives of the local and central administrations, and those of the unions, experts on the issue of immigration, and representatives of the third sector. It is seen as an important action that appreciates the active role that foreigners have within the scope of the third sector.

Another very important requisite in order to be able to speak of integration, and thus of membership and citizenship, is language. Learning, knowing, and speaking the language is in fact an absolutely fundamental requirement necessary for social inclusion. The knowledge of the language (for young people who came to Italy for family reunification) is the first step to enable communication and social relations. Language does not mean just words and concepts, but also proverbs and popular sayings, symbols rich in emotional meaning. The family often exerts pressure in favour of maintaining the language of origin, a clear sign of the bond and the preservation of their cultural roots: the loss of language might mean the loss of identity of their cultural roots (Villano & Zani, 2004). In many cases, however, the children feel the need to abandon their native language for the benefit of a second language, perceived as a tool to facilitate their acceptance/*l'accettazione* by native peers. Not paying attention to this fundamental aspect poses a risk to young migrants: the attitude marginal (margin), which breathes life into the limits of both the culture of origin and that of destination, with a rejection of the conduct of the new reality and those of their group, is the worst strategy of acculturation, because it often generates feelings of defeat and failure and is an inadequate defence, which is not functional in terms of a personal identity and social inclusion. This closed position towards the new can be negative for the formation of identity, because we know that comparison with peers is an essential element for the construction of the personal and the social.

The issue of civic participation of young migrants involves several key points. In the words of the Member of Parliament interviewed, participation means:

> knowledge of the rights and duties that can be correctly enjoyed and respected at the time when the subject is able to become aware of them, and from here the effort of our administration (that is the Ministry for Employment and Social Policies) has been to foster the access to this knowledge by means of a campaign of communication on social integration.

The targets of this information campaign were first young Italians. It sought to sensitize them to migrants' contribution to the country through their work and economic and social growth. The secondary targets of the campaign were migrants with the aim of transferring information and knowledge with respect to the fundamental norms of the national juridical system:

> We have not only made some commercials, but also some actions on the territory where multilingual guides were distributed (in eight languages, Italian, English, French, Spanish, Arab, Chinese, Russian and Albanian, that is the nationalities most of all present in Italy), that started with a first part on the Italian constitution, then access to services, how to register a child at school, how to open a current account. This was done in the light of providing the instruments, above all for those who have recently arrived in this country.

This is an important attempt at the civic involvement of migrants, but still far from those forms of social inclusion that would make people real citizens. In Italy, the main emergency relating to migration is not about social inclusion, but rather about border and territory controls, in addition to concerns that are generated owing to the pressure exerted on the labour market and welfare systems, not to mention changes in the composition of ethnic, linguistic, and cultural identity and social cohesion.

The projects involved are mostly regional or municipal initiatives, or NGOs working in the field. As suggested by Colombo (2012), currently it seems that there is no convergence of European countries towards similar policies on migration or an attempt by the European Union to play a central and leading role in integration policies. Europe, according to the interviewees, represents 'a pool from which to draw funds (without which informational campaigns cannot be started)', even if it is perceived as 'something that is still top-down, where the technical component is strong and instead there is a lack of spirit. The work that is done with the new generations is thus important'.

In spite of this 'distance' from Europe—denounced by the MP in the narrative on the young people—with respect to the issue of immigration, our interviewee argues that the EU has incorporated (by inserting them in the work agenda the 2009 Stockholm

Programme) some of the Italian proposals, such as the importance of legal immigration and the safeguarding of the unaccompanied foreign minors. Italy is moving in harmony with the EU in regard to the intensification of the cooperation policies with countries from which the migrants come (for example, Libya and Albania). Related measures include:

- Bilateral agreements on the subject of work.
- Cooperation on the front of regular immigration, which means the reinforcement of the entrance channels to limit the illegal arrivals. Italy and the European Union are working on the integration indices (that is, a set of indicators—accommodation, work, language, health—for the evaluation of the policies and measures for the integration of the migrants).
- Enforcement of specific projects *in loco* for the creation in these countries of lists of foreign workers available to come to Italy to work.

Our interviewee, however, is also careful about the future prospects, claiming that all these policies can, however, only be implemented if we invest in the young generations in order to strengthen and consolidate this sense of membership, because it is in these terms that we can accomplish that common sentiment. Otherwise the EU will always be seen as something top-down that in very many cases can even enter into an antithesis with the local and national interests. According to the representatives of two NGOs (Cospe—Cooperation for the Development of the Emerging Countries—and Nexus[6]), the fundamental priorities in relation to social policies for migrants are integration and social participation. The latter is understood as broad, cultural, and innovative participation—not only participation in associations—and above all inclusion in the labour market. Indeed, it is not accidental that among the priorities highlighted by the projects undertaken by the NGOs are the right to work, understood as the 'construction of pathways of cooperation for development that have work at their heart' (E.P. Cospe); the right to an identity (legal), understood as the contemporary value of their ethnic values and adaptation to the new reality, which leads to well-being and satisfaction (Berry, 1997); and the right to training and the possibility of a large opening towards the new culture, its knowledge, and the possibility of promotion.

Other important issues emerging from the interviews relate to the incentive structure for migrants' participation in and contribution to the labour market. Political participation arises from a wider engagement with the social and economic life of the country. Three issues are identified as key to social inclusion: access to citizenship rights, clear rules relating to residency, and investment in development activities. The quotes below illustrate the nature of the discourse and highlight the role of these organizations in promoting migrants' participation:

> Without the vote there are no rights, because it empowers them not only to express and therefore participate, in spite of the fact that they are, for other aspects, citizens with full rights: when it comes to paying taxes, paying healthcare fees, contributing to the pensions that are more ours than theirs, they are citizens in every respect. When instead it comes to counting in the country's political life, hence civil life, they are not given the right to vote. And this means not having their own representatives. (S.P. President of NEXUS—Cooperation and Solidarity—Emilia Romagna)

The right to vote is thus singled out as critical to enhance the quality of migrant citizenship.

The residency rules and difficulties in gaining the 'right to remain' are the main obstacles to the participation of migrants in Italian social and political life. In the words of the representative of Cospe:

> The lack of a norm on the inflows is the true problem. If I do not have a permit of stay I can do nothing; there is a block that generates basic structural discrimination. If I do not have the permit of stay I struggle to participate in the labour market, because I only participate in the illegal or clandestine labour market. So a whole series of measures made at the government level that have also been made by the previous governments to allow people to enter Italy with some really regular flows.

A complex picture starts to emerge. Government departments' and civil society organizations' positions on social inclusion of migrants share a common concern with integration, yet the focus on residency and access highlights the impact of current policies on maintaining the marginal role of these groups.

So what does Europe represent for the representatives of civil society organizations? The NGO representatives interviewed portray a very mixed vision of Europe. NGOs are particularly critical of the Italian government's approach to immigration if disassociated from a broader European vision (but note that the interviews took place before Kashetu's appointment in 2013 as Minister for International Cooperation and Integration). After the 2009 Treaty of Lisbon the only really common field among the various European countries are border controls: NGO projects make up for this gap through information networks that have generated exchange of good practices. This process can help migrants experiencing difficulties. In this context, it is clear that the NGOs' assessment of the EU's role in promoting citizenship and participation is rather negative:

> Europe does not exist, there exist single countries: there is no Charter of Rights recognized by all the countries. We can say that the European policy of promotion of citizenship is the sum of the policies that the individual countries carry out. There is no single policy that sees all of the European countries in agreement on the theme of immigration. (member of Cospe)

Europe's role in promoting migrants' political rights is thus key to challenging the dominant discourse of participation, engagement, and migrants' integration in the host community.

Conclusions

In this review of Italian legislation and civil society projects, one element links together all the concepts: citizenship is and must be a common asset, an asset that can characterize each person and each society in a deep and responsible manner. Whether we are speaking of young people or migrants, we need to think that being citizens means essentially being free: to travel, to work, to vote, to take part in the life of one's city, and to think. Being citizens means feeling like an important part of the country in which one decides to live, to feel listened to and worthy of consideration or what we are and what we do.

Only that way can we speak of social inclusion. And all of this must start from training, education, and school. Indeed, the training processes, 'the transformations of the relationships inside and outside the institutions, such as being collectively organized to enter the public space, all represent attempts to construct citizenship enforced in everyday social life' (Guerzoni & Riccio, 2009, p. 11).

What transpires from the interviews is a general concern with the decline in manifest civic and political engagement. The danger is that the principles of citizenship could become devoid of meaning and traction. In order for these principles to maintain their position of primacy in political discourse, all citizens need to be encouraged to take ownership of these fundamental values at the heart of the relationship with the state. The psychosocial literature shows that moral values can motivate people, for example, towards political commitment, such as the vote (Stika, 2008).

In conclusion, what emerges from looking at the political participation of young people is an increasing awareness that many are oriented towards other forms of participation (perhaps more indirect and subtle), thus signalling a rejection of traditional forms of participation and engagement. Some research in this direction shows that in fact the experience of ineffectiveness and powerlessness related to experiences of direct political participation discourages civic and political engagement (Zani *et al.*, 2011).

Among the migrants, however, the desire to integrate and participate in political and civic Italian life is present, but collides with the obstacle of the absence of the right of citizenship, on which the political world seems to turn a deaf ear. In addition, work commitments and economic and cultural difficulties do not favour the active involvement of migrants.

So what can be done? We need more positive discourse on young people and for young people, centred on their potential and resources, where they are considered to be active participants. This is the premise for any real change in policies on young people and migrants. And we need to think about participation policies that not only promote the active participation and the involvement of young people through a real partnership between youth and adults, but also enhance the latent forms of engagement and participation that we saw most present in the experiences of youth and migrants.

And Europe? Europe is still distant from Italy and Italian policies, especially on young people and migrants. Prodi (2003) claims that one of the main complaints raised against the EU is the overarching failure of its institutions to communicate the values and principles underpinning the project. The distance between the people of Europe and its institutions continues to undermine processes for engagement and participation, especially between youth. A constant preoccupation of both civil society organizations and political actors is the issue of multiple loyalties.

As Nussbaum (2010) claims, our task is to develop an intelligent citizenship, a political sustainability that recognizes all the existing groups and their needs, as well as their rights and duties. Europe, in its enlargement, has experienced a moment of great progress and enthusiasm. In Italy we need a full recognition of the rights of all the groups and the individuals that are a part of it and an improvement of communication between the political representatives and young people and migrants, so that they can actually feel their closeness and responsiveness and can feel listened to and taken into account.

Notes

1. The four referenda ask the Italian public to vote on issues relating to water supply (two referendums), nuclear power, and 'legittimo impedimento' (in Italian criminal law, the possibility for the defendant not to appear in court because of concomitant political commitments).
2. http://epp.eurostat.ec.europa.eu/.
3. Ministry for the Interior, Ministry for Youth Policies, Ministry of Education and Further and Higher Education, 'Ermes' that is the portal of the Emilia Romagna region, Portal for Immigration of the Veneto Region, the ISMU Foundation, website of the Observatory on Immigration Piedmont Region; website of the Observatory for Integration and Multi-ethnicity of the Lombardy Region.
4. The National Civil Service became a specific and independent service starting from 1 January 2005 with the suspension of compulsory conscription pursuant to Law no. 266 passed on 23 August 2004.
5. Seventh Framework Programme, FP7-SSH-2007-1, Grant Agreement no: 225282, Processes Influencing Democratic Ownership and Participation (PIDOP). Partners: University of Surrey (UK), University of Liège (Belgium), Masaryk University (Czech Republic), University of Jena (Germany), University of Bologna (Italy), University of Porto (Portugal), Örebro University (Sweden), Ankara University (Turkey), and Queen's University Belfast (UK).
6. Nexus is an institute for development cooperation promoted by CGIL Emilia Romagna. Set up in 1993, it was recognized as an NGO by the Ministry for Foreign Affairs in 2007.

References

Amnå, E. (2010) Active passive or standby citizens? Latent and manifest political participation, in: E. Amnå, (Ed.) *New Form of Citizen Participation: Normative Implications*, pp. 191–203 (Baden-Baden: Nomos).

Anderson, M. R. (2010) Community psychology political efficacy and trust, *Political Psychology*, 31(1), pp. 59–84.

Bee, C. & Scartezzini, R. (2009) *La Costruzione Sociale dell'Europa. Processi di Europeizzazione della Società Civile* [The Social Construction of Europe. Processes of Europeanisation of Civil Society] (Soveria Mannelli: Rubettino Editore).

Berry, J. W. (1997) Immigration, acculturation, and adaptation, *Applied Psychology*, 46(1), pp. 5–34.

Claibourne, M. P. & Martin, P. A. (2002) Trusting and joining? An empirical test of the reciprocal nature of social capital, *Political Behavior*, 22(4), pp. 267–91.

Colombo, A. D. (2012) *Fuori Controllo? Miti e Realtà dell'immigrazione in Italia* [Out of Control? Myths and Reality of Immigration in Italy] (Bologna: Il Mulino).

Cuconato, M., De Luigi, N. & Martelli, A. (2012) Youth participation in the framework of the reformulation of local youth policies in Italy, in: P. Loncle, M. Cuconato, V. Muniglia & A. Walther (Eds) *Youth Participation in Europe. Beyond Discourses, Practices and Realities*, pp. 93–108 (Bristol: The Policy Press).

Ekman, I. & Amnå, E. (2009) Political participation and civic engagement: Toward a new typology, *Youth & Society, Working Paper, 2*, Department of Social and Political Sciences, Örebro University, Sweden.

Entman, R. M. (1993) Framing: Toward clarification of a fractured paradigm, *Journal of Communication*, 43(4), pp. 51–58.

European Commission. (2013) *Co-creating European Union Citizenship* (Luxembourg: Publications Office of the European Union).

Guerzoni, G. & Riccio, B. (2009) *Giovani in Cerca di cittadinanza* [Young People Seeking Citizenship] (Rimini: Guaraldi Universitaria).

Kosic, A. (2007) Motivation for civic participation of immigrants: The role of personal resources, social identities, and personal traits, *POLITIS-Working Paper No.11/2007*, University of Oldenburg. Available at http://www.uni-oldenburg.de/politis-europe/webpublications

La Due Lake, R. & Huckfeldt, R. (1998) Social capital social networks and participation, *Political Psychology*, 19(3), pp. 567–584.

Loncle, P., Cuconato, M., Muniglia, V. & Walther, A. (2012) *Youth Participation in Europe. Beyond Discourses, Practices and Realities* (Bristol: The Policy Press).

Martin, I. & van Deth, J. W. (2007) Political involvement in citizenship involvement, in: L. J. W. van Deth, J. R. Montero & A. Westholm (Eds) *European Democracies: A Comparative Analysis*, pp. 303–33 (London and New York: Routledge).

McMillan, D. & Chavis, D. (1986) Sense of community: A definition and theory, *Journal of Community Psychology*, 14, pp. 6–23.
Mesa, D. (2010) Le politiche giovanili in Italia: attori, prospettive e modelli di intervento, *Autonomie Locali e Servizi Sociali*, 2, pp. 261–74.
Nussbaum, M. (2010) *Not for Profit. Why Democracy Needs the Humanities* (Princeton, NJ: Princeton University Press).
Prodi, R. (2003) Educazione e Cultura, in: P. Bertolini (Ed.) *Educazione e Politica* [Education and Politics], pp. 3–12 (Milano: Raffaello Cortina).
Putnam, R. D. (1993) *Making Democracy Work* (Princeton, NJ: Princeton University Press).
Putnam, R. D. (1995) Bowling alone, *Journal of Democracy*, 6(65), pp. 65–78.
Sciolla, L. (2004) *La sfida dei valori: rispetto delle regole e rispetto dei diritti in Italia*, Vol. 533 (Bologna: Il Mulino).
Smirnov-Brkíc, A., Christopoulos, M., Karakosta, K., Martinez Bermejo, S., & Reboton, J. (2010) Milestones in the development of the concept of citizenship, in: K. Isaaks (Ed.) *Citizenship and Identities: Inclusion Exclusion Participation*, pp. 2–12 (Pisa: Pisa University Press).
Stika, L. J. (2008) Moral conviction and political engagement, *Political Psychology*, 29(1), pp. 29–54.
Teorell, J., Torcal, M. & Montero, J. R. (2007) Political participation: Mapping the terrain, in: J. W. van Deth, J. R. Montero & A. Westholm (Eds) *Citizenship and Involvement in European Democracies: A Comparative Analysis*, pp. 334–357 (London and New York: Routledge).
Theiss-Morse, E. (1993) Conceptualizations of good citizenship and political participation, *Political Behavior*, 15(4), pp. 355–380.
Villano, P. & Zani, B. (2004) Donne forti, *Psicologia Contemporanea*, 185, pp. 34–41.
Zani, B., Cicognani, E. & Albanesi, C. (2011) *La Partecipazione Civica e Politica dei giovani. Discorsi, Esperienze, Significati* [The Civic and Political Participation of Young People. Discourses, Experiences, Meanings] (Bologna: Clueb).

Active Citizenship in the UK: Assessing Institutional Political Strategies and Mechanisms of Civic Engagement

CRISTIANO BEE* & DIMITRA PACHI**

*School of Politics, University of Surrey, Guildford, UK; **School of Psychology, University of Surrey, Guildford, UK

ABSTRACT *Shaping active citizenship, motivating civic engagement, and increasing political participation of minority groups have become some of the key political priorities in the UK since at least the end of the 1980s. Academic research shows that this shift goes hand-in-hand with a review of the integration policies in the country. The 'politics of integration' correspond in fact to a policy response to various social problems (such as discrimination, racism, intolerance) that emerged in various areas, and represent a new political discourse regarding active citizenship. This reflects an overall strategy meant to reframe the basis for civic and political engagement and participation in Britain. Our article is thus meant to highlight the dynamics underlying the development of the concept of active citizenship in the UK by looking at the factors that intervene in its shaping and enhancement. We identify political priorities and key mechanisms of participation that enable engagement in the public sphere. This article first considers the development of the specific 'British discourse' regarding active citizenship by taking into consideration the political priorities that emerged as part of the New Right discourse in the 1980s and then New Labour after 1997. We then refer to a set of data collected during our field work conducted in the UK between 2010 and 2011 with civil society activists and policy-makers in order to underline the meaning, practices, and feasibility of active citizenship.*

Introduction

Although traditionally perceived as a bond between the political community and the individual, the concept of citizenship has transformed across time due to a number of reasons and processes which have challenged its understanding. Under question is the link with the nation state and its institutions and the idea that 'citizenship mediates interactions between individuals and the state' (Drake, 2001, p. 119). The concept has also been challenged by a number of processes (such as Europeanization, globalization, and devolution) that have emerged and shaped the public realm. The debate addresses the relationship between the individual and the political community, as well as the broader interconnections between individuals and social groups (Faulks, 2000). Therefore the concept of citizenship as a social idea implies a sense of obligation with other members of a community, as well as an understanding of the role and the contribution of the individual in that specific community. Furthermore, centrally debated in the social policy literature are the relationship and the weight of the rights and obligations that citizenship entails. The article addresses these issues fitting in the contemporary broader scholarly debate in citizenship studies (Lister, 1997; Heater, 1999; *Castles & Davidson, 2000*; Eder & Giesen, 2001; Bellamy et al., 2004; Delanty, 2007; Miller, 2008a). More precisely it takes inspiration from the confrontation and comparison of two models of citizenship that emerged in the literature, the neoliberal and the civic republican ones. In this context, we discuss the peculiarities of the British approach to active citizenship by looking first at differences in policy discourse that emerged over time and are grounded on different ideological standpoints and by then presenting the results of the field work that we conducted.

More specifically, the aim of this article is to outline the trends that have been driving conceptualizations of citizenship and the practice of active citizenship in Britain. First, we frame the definitions of citizenship and active citizenship in light of the debate regarding different political philosophies, in order to account for the main differences between them. Second, in order to contextualize the debate on active citizenship, we address the citizenship reform promoted under the New Right governments of Margaret Thatcher and John Major between the end of the 1980s and the beginning of the 1990s. We then progress into a discussion of the characteristics assumed by 'active citizenship' in the politics of the New Labour's government initiated by Tony Blair in 1997. In line with the research objectives of the processes influencing democratic ownership and participation (PIDOP) project that focused specifically on the active engagement of traditionally marginalized groups, we discuss New Labour's approach to active citizenship by taking a particular angle, which is the one of integration policy. Finally, we outline some general findings based on policy analysis of 37 policy documents published by public institutions and nongovernmental organizations (NGOs) in Britain in the period 2005–2010 and from six interviews conducted with NGO activists in 2011.

The aim of this analysis is to provide insights into the core policy values and objectives of the NGOs and to assess the overall discourses regarding the policies of active engagement and citizenship under New Labour. The arguments and analysis presented in this article are part of the multidisciplinary project PIDOP that produced a comparative analysis of policies of civic engagement and citizenship in eight European countries. In this regard, the British discourse on active citizenship provides a valuable evidence base for comparative purposes with the rest of the articles in this special issue.

Framing Definitions of Citizenship: Ideological Traditions

Two traditional ideological viewpoints on citizenship, namely the liberal (and neoliberal) and the civic republican, have influenced the political setting of different European countries and resulted in different models of balance between two core components, rights and responsibilities, and also for the overall practices that this status entails (Delanty, 2000, 2007; Bellamy et al., 2004; Miller, 2008b; Carrera & Guild, 2009; Isin et al., 2009). While the neoliberal perspective of citizenship accounts for a 'passive citizen' and the rights that are ensured in order to guarantee the expression of certain freedoms, the civic republican perspective refers to an 'active citizen' and the reciprocal responsibilities that members of a political community have towards each other.

The neoliberal perspective is based upon the idea of citizenship as a status, based on a negative notion of freedom, favouring the individual over the community and emphasizing a broad set of rights guaranteed by the state. In Britain, insights on the debate regarding the shaping of the neoliberal model of citizenship are provided in the classic work by Marshall (1950), where it is argued that the rights of citizenship have evolved across time to include civil, political, and social rights. Marshall argues that social rights have been included first because they guarantee a minimum set of standards that ensure social cohesion and second because they make the expression of civil and political rights significant. It also needs to be emphasized that the neoliberal definition of citizenship has been subjected to a number of criticisms in the literature (Pateman, 1988; Lister, 1997; Heater, 1999).

The emergence of cultural and minority rights has received much attention in a first strand of literature that has evaluated the neoliberal model. Critiques of Marshall (Lister, 1997; Stevenson, 2001) highlight a lack of understanding of the complexity of society and failure to fully account for the issue of difference. In her work, Lister (1997, 2007) addresses the historical process of exclusion of women from the exercise of their political rights until a good part of the twentieth century. Advocates for the inclusion of minority rights have played a central role in transforming the concept of citizenship across time, arguing that the denial of difference that characterizes the neoliberal model of citizenship has led to the oppression of minorities. Young (1990) also looks at the lack of accounting for diversity in Western society, which is sacrificed in the name of an abstract and unattainable conception of citizenship; she argues for the necessity of shaping politics of difference where group identities are incorporated into the decision-making institutions of the community, advocating for a differentiated citizenship built upon group rights.

In his work Kymlicka (1995) also criticizes another of the main principles of Marshall's conceptualization of citizenship, that of universalism, for the reason that it renders cultural minorities vulnerable to significant injustice at the hands of the majority and exacerbates ethno-cultural conflicts because of the fragmentation it creates. He has argued for the integration of selective principles, in particular group differentiated rights. This discussion is central to our article, because the redefinition of the concept of citizenship occurring in the UK under New Labour has been widely influenced by this recognition of the importance of minority rights and issues of difference that characterize multicultural Britain (Phillimore, 2012).

A second strand of literature has argued for a 'communitarian citizenship'. Neo-communitarianism, as it is called, represents a critique of the individualism in Western society caused by neoliberal politics. This constitutes a political and intellectual discourse that first appeared in the USA with the work of Taylor (1989) and Walzer (1983) and represents 'a critical response to Reaganite market neo-liberalism' (Marinetto, 2003, p. 107). As part of this critique, communitarians (Etzioni, 1993, 1995) point out the importance of social interactions of the individual in social groups, of the role of informal networks for revitalizing the sense of community and civic life, and the role played by cultural and political identity in order to reach a common good.

Elements of criticism of the neoliberal perspective also become evident when we compare it with the civic republican perspective on citizenship. According to the civic republican perspective (Bellamy, 2000; Miller, 2000), citizenship is a civic virtue that entails the individual's active participation in the political and social life and his/her full integration in the community (see also Mouffe, 1992). Miller (2000) also refers to a model of neo-republican citizenship in which individuals, in addition to having a set of rights and obligations, are also active in shaping common interests, are committed to protecting the rights of others in the political community, and are actively participating in policy-making. Deliberative democracy is central to this tradition.

Habermas widely argues in his work that the citizen acts, expresses concerns, develops opinions, and shapes policies with his/her participation in the public sphere (Habermas, 1994, 1996). The expression of a civic identity in the public sphere is thus central and accounts for the citizen being an active political actor rather than a passive one. It is worth emphasizing here that Habermas's account of the public sphere and his interpretation of the emergence and value of a bourgeois public sphere have been widely criticized. Fraser (1992), for example, argues that Habermas ignores the existence of counter-publics (such as women and/or minorities), who are excluded from the public domain and struggle for their voice to be heard. This is an important point to be taken into consideration, because as we will argue later when discussing our findings, it is an emerging discourse that provides criticism of New Labour's style of active citizenship. This in fact, even though stressing the importance of bottom-up processes of participation, is not yet perceived by NGO activists as fully inclusive of traditionally marginalized groups.

It can thus be argued that the theoretical debate regarding active citizenship is contextually framed within the civic republican account of citizenship and is common to a number of Western countries. It is also connected to broader themes, such as the best ways to deliver rights and entitlements, the balance between duties and responsibilities, the emergence of participatory systems of public policy, the strengthening of the role of the civil society in policy-making, and the assumptions of new roles by local governments with the consequence of strengthening the communitarian dimension. Although this theoretical perspective addresses the mechanisms that may encourage public participation and civic engagement, it remains open to interpretation when considered from alternative ideological standpoints.

Marinetto (2003) explained the emergence of the debate on active citizenship in the 1980s in the Western world with reference to the existing fragmentation between right-wing and left-wing ideologies. In that time context, two opposite definitions of active citizenship emerged:

> Protagonists of the right emphasized the importance of promoting active citizenship to achieve a balance between rights and duties. This was seen as a logical extension of the prevailing political orthodoxy of the time which sought to reduce the burden of state and introduce greater private sector provision of public goods. (Marinetto, 2003, p. 107)

Based on neoliberal roots, the concept of active citizenship put forward by right-wing politicians was aimed at preserving and promoting individual liberty by enhancing a sense of utilitarian responsibility towards the community. Social democratic viewpoints addressed instead the emergence of active citizenship from a different point, looking at the broader civic involvement of the individual in a given community: 'People on the centre left also took up the question of active citizenship for quite different reasons. Their concern was to defend the collective fabric of public life against encroachment by the market' (Marinetto, 2003, p. 107). As we will see in the next two sections, these ideological arguments characterize the shaping of active citizenship in modern Britain as well.

The Emergence of 'Active Citizenship' in the New Right Political Discourse

The role of the individual within the community and his/her relationship with state institutions have characterized the debate on active citizenship in Britain since at least the end of the 1980s. The discussion is particularly relevant because it reflects the 'ideological struggle for control over the meaning of citizenship' (Smith, 1995, p. 190) that entailed a confrontation between political philosophies put forward by coalitions holding power in different time contexts. Therefore, this debate is especially interesting given that issues of engagement and participation were at the time politically and socially at the forefront of the conservative policies of Thatcher and Major and also subsequently central to the New Labour ideology of Tony Blair. As Brehony (1992, p. 203) argues, '1988 was another vintage year for the discovery, or rediscovery, of citizenship as a solution to perceived problems both social and political'. In declaring that

> greater opportunities for active citizens are being offered and taken up (...) our action against crime and against drugs relies increasingly on a partnership between statutory agencies, the relevant professions and public-spirited citizens. (Hurd cited in Faulks, 1998, p. 128)

Douglas Hurd, Home Secretary at the time, launched the neoliberal style of active citizenship in Britain, expressing a commitment, consequently shaped and renewed in John Major's government between 1990 and 1997.

Active citizenship, according to Hurd, entailed the following:

> (...) involvement in charitable work and voluntary groups—for example, through neighbourhood watch and victim support schemes (...). There is a need for even closer partnership between the public, private and voluntary sectors. I have been having and will continue to have discussions with representatives of all three sectors in order to identify and publicise ways in which people can turn concern into effective voluntary action. (Hurd, 1989)

This definition of active citizenship has at least three characteristics. First of all, it is contextual to the need to foster new values at the community level in order to face new emerging social problems (Keith, 1989; Faulks, 1998; Marinetto, 2003; Davies, 2012). At the same time, it attempts to foster a notion of active citizenship based on a renewed approach to local governance favoured by an enhanced engagement of civil society through voluntary action (MacKian, 1995; Marston, 1995). Third, it enhances citizens' reciprocal responsibility, in order to challenge dependency effects that, according to conservatives, are caused by Marshall's model of citizenship (Heater, 1991; Oliver, 1991; Roche, 1992).

In one of the many academic writings and policy analyses produced at the time, Brehony (1992, p. 203) assessed this set of policy initiatives by locating the attempt to foster active citizenship as being in line with the civic republican tradition. However, this interpretation was met with subsequent criticism, with many scholars arguing that this approach to active citizenship had prominent neoliberal connotations (see, e.g. Oliver, 1991; Fyfe, 1993, 1995). As documented by a number of scholars (Faulks, 1998; Kearns, 1995), the New Right approach to active citizenship was far from being open and based on participatory means. The 'active citizenship campaign' is considered to be coherent with the neoliberal politics of the conservative government at the time and based on the need to foster a sense of individual responsibility among the citizens.

In this regard, as argued by Faulks (1998, p. 128), the notion of active citizenship that was taken forward was that of 'a dynamic individual who was self-reliant, responsible for his or her own actions, and yet possessed a sense of civic virtue and pride both in country and local community'. The sense of involvement in local issues, through participation in voluntary work and the sharing of common values, was therefore centrally orienting the New Right approach. In interpreting this, Faulks (1998, p. 128) continues by arguing that

> the active citizenship campaign was consistent with the Neoliberal agenda of Thatcherism, which was concerned more with the development of a citizenship based upon the assertion of the individual and the market, rather than a genuine concern for the promotion of community values.

On this account, Oliver (1991, p. 164) argues that the conservatives' vision about citizenship was one-dimensional, consisting of a set of obligations, which a citizen owes to the community.

In order to understand the conceptualization of active citizenship at the time, we need to interpret it in conjunction with another important initiative, the Citizens Charter launched by Major in 1991. The Charter respects the principles of active citizenship promoted by the Conservative political discourse by purporting to establish for citizens better access to public services, the need for public services to operate efficiently, and the guarantee of a higher degree of choice for citizens based on new market mechanisms (Fyfe, 1993). This programme of reforms aimed at a more efficient provision of public services and is to be interpreted along with programmes such as the 1988 and 1993 Education Act, the 1988 House and Local Government Act, and the 1990 National Health Service and Community Care Act. All these, as Faulks (1998, p. 133) explained, were attempts to 'increase personal responsibility and the basic market right of the citizen' by promoting a consumerist culture. Furthermore, Kearns (1995, p. 160) underlined the fact that the Charter 'diverts the citizens' energies into complaints to the service provider rather than into an engagement with, or involvement in, governance'.

It can thus be argued that a change in the role and functions of the public administration with a growing role given to the local authorities was central at the time. This process principally entailed 'openings for the active citizen to exercise power and influence within a pluralist system for devising collective strategies and providing public services' (Kearns, 1995, p. 159), and implied an opening to the third sector, with a more prominent role given to voluntary organizations (Brehony, 1992). However, in commenting upon this expansion of concern regarding the local dimension, Kearns (1995, p. 159) argued that 'it is the upper middle and professional classes who will be expected to exercise control within a range of new or expanded governmental and nongovernmental organisations'.

This consideration is central in the overall critique of the New Right style of active citizenship, highlighting that the neoliberal politics of the Thatcher and Major governments were enhancing social divisions at the community level rather than creating principles and values allowing for conditions of social solidarity to foster the actual exercise of active citizenship. At the time, this was considered to emerge from the need to provide individual responsibility in order to contrast the shared dependency culture driving the welfare state in the post-WWII period. Moreover it was oriented towards the preservation of individual liberty rather than towards actual engagement with community life (Faulks, 1998, p. 130). Overall, instead of favouring better civic engagement with politics, the notion of active citizenship that was put forward was not politicized and entailed neither empowerment in the political community nor actual involvement in the public sphere. It can therefore be argued that 'the Conservative's active citizen is apolitical' (Oliver, 1991, p. 165) and that the principles favoured were thus not those of a public that participates, protests, or dissents, but rather of 'a politically uninterested public' (Kearns, 1995, p. 160).

New Labour, Active Citizenship, and Community Cohesion: Policy Responses to Integration Policy

The shift in government with New Labour as the leading party in Britain was characterized by a renewed commitment on the issue and definition of active citizenship and was characterized by the political necessity to make 'community a central political theme' (Marinetto, 2003, p. 114). The Labour government, and in particular the Home Secretary David Blunkett, shaped a new public policy agenda based on a civil renewal (see NCVO, 2005, p. 3) supported by specific integrated policy actions aimed at strengthening three interconnected areas: active citizenship (through, e.g. citizenship education, raising community participation through volunteering work, and enhancing civic participation and engagement with state institutions), strengthening communities (through the interconnection of the dimensions of community development, through community cohesion, and community safety), and enhancing partnership in meeting public needs (through the enhancement of participation in local decision-making and through support to non-state organizations in the delivery of public services). Participatory democracy and civic engagement were thus central in the political discourse of New Labour, marking therefore a substantial difference with the conservatives' notion that, as aforementioned, did not account for the politicization of active citizenship. In fact, during this time period the government put forward a new set of ideas and provided evidence of a 'commitment to extending public involvement in the policy making and democratic process' (Marinetto, 2003, p. 116).

In the New Labour political discourse, issues such as civic engagement, active citizenship, and civil society at the local level were central in order to shape forms of collective action allowing for increased participation in policy processes. The aims of the 'Third Way' were to create stronger ties between the private and public sectors and to facilitate the development of public/private partnerships. The centrality of these ideas in promoting an active sense of citizenship has widely been remarked upon by Giddens (1998, 2000,

2001). In rethinking the process of change that undermines the welfare state, he points at the emergence of a positive welfare based on a stronger commitment and partnership between public institutions and civil society (Giddens, 2006).

Community engagement and empowerment were thus established as policy priorities in this scenario and were promoted through a wide set of policies by New Labour (Worley, 2005). A meaningful example of this is the New Deal for Communities programme, established in order to challenge social exclusion and to raise engagement in 39 areas all around the UK and run from 1998 to 2008. It aimed at strengthening bottom-up processes of involvement and engagement of local communities and particularly deprived neighbourhoods. Participation in community building represented attempts to generate forms of community ownership 'enabling people to respond to, and take advantage of their opportunities' (Brannan et al., 2006, p. 1000). Assessments have applauded this framework because of the bottom-up dynamics underlining this programme, based on injecting and promoting principles of participatory governance (see Atkinson, 2003; Dinam, 2005; Wright, et al., 2006), but at the same time have widely criticized its establishment because of the actual limitations caused by a highly 'idealised notion of participation in democratic institutions' (Wright et al., 2006 p. 355). Overall, as we argue in the next section, our data provide confirmation of this insofar as actual involvement in policy-making processes is not perceived as being fully inclusive by the activists that we interviewed.

The shaping of active citizenship under New Labour is also linked with the emergence of new social problems that have resulted in academic and institutional reflection on the reframing of integration policies. This discussion, we believe, is particularly important, since one of the core objectives of the PIDOP project was to investigate the mechanisms fostering civic engagement and democratic ownership by traditionally marginalized groups. A wide set of literature describes how New Labour policies have brought into the agenda the need to provide policy responses to address new emerging social problems afflicting British society (McGhee, 2003; Robinson, 2005; Burnett, 2007; Modood, 2007; Mulvey, 2010). As documented in the work of McGhee (2003, 2006, 2008, 2009), clashes between communities in Oldham, Burnley and Bradford in 2001 and then the terrorist attack of 7/7 in London in 2005 were at the basis of a number of policy responses to the fragmentation of British society as it emerged at the end of the 1990s. This essentially put into question the basis of a multicultural society. The New Labour agenda therefore fit with this new emerging context in which 'disturbances spawned an industry with the agenda of enhancing citizenship, increasing integration and building community cohesion' (McGhee, 2009, p. 45). This emphasis on the lack of integration and the separation between communities was expressed with a series of policy actions taken forward by New Labour governments between 2001 and 2010 and was characterized by a 'model of civic assimilation based on the idea of forging allegiance to core principles shared by all through the effective engagement of responsible 'active citizens' located in 'active communities' (McGhee, 2009, p. 49).

In the 2001 *Report of the Independent Review Team* on social cohesion, it was stated that it was

> essential to establish a greater sense of citizenship, based on (a few) common principles which are shared and observed by all sections of the community. This concept of citizenship would also place a higher value on cultural differences. (Home Office, 2001, p. 10)

This resulted in British public institutions becoming more self-reflecting on issues of cultural pluralism, the issue of difference, and the inclusion of a number of minorities in the definition of citizenship. In 2002 the *Secure Borders, Safe Haven* White Paper, for example, put forward the necessity to think more closely along the civic dimension of citizenship (Home Office, 2002).

A number of policy documents developed during this time help us to understand the centrality of active citizenship and community cohesion for building a new approach to integration policy in Britain. However, in evaluating these policy responses, Ratcliffe (2012, p. 275) underlines that 'the New Labour government remained, at least, somewhat equivocal on the relationship between equality and (community) cohesion'. McGhee underlines how these strategies were actually biased because they were not integrative in the full sense but more closely looking at the adaptation and assimilation of minorities. In his evaluation of New Labour's policies McGhee (2006, p. 118) states that they neglected 'a balanced integration strategy for both potential "host" communities and "new" migrants. At the same time, the strategy of deterrence has had the unintended consequence of legitimizing racism and asylophobia in Britain'. The data that we report below provide evidence that the approach put forward by New Labour was actually based on a one-way model of civic engagement based on assimilationist principles. As McGhee (2009, p. 51) further explains:

> The focus of Home Secretary David Blunkett's citizenship strategy was less on the deliberative quality of identities forged (and modified) in interaction with others than on a rather more "practical" intervention in which basic skills (English language proficiency and a superficial "knowledge of life in the UK") become the means whereby civic responsibilities can be taken up.

First, the events of the 7/7 London bombings and then the shift in government from Blair to Brown produced a shift in the policies of active citizenship. The strengthening of the assimilationist approach as well as the shaping of 'Britishness' as a core value for minority groups are expressed by the approach taken towards citizenship after 2005. As the Home Secretary Jacqui Smith expressed in her Foreword to the 2008 Green Paper, *The Path to Citizenship,* the aim was to base integration policies on a 'journey to citizenship' (Home Office, 2008, p. 5).

The three-stage journey (temporary residence, probationary citizenship, and British citizenship/permanent residence) proposed in the Green Paper is meant to set the requirement to earn citizenship and the right to stay in the UK. This is marked as a core principle in the section of the Green Paper dedicated to Active Citizenship:

> We tested the idea of asking newcomers to participate in some kind of community work. For many in the discussions this was an important idea—in particular for the contribution it could make to better integrated communities. It was generally thought to be an idea that should be implemented as early as possible in the migrant's journey into the UK, and it was seen as a positive way in which newcomers could demonstrate a commitment to Britain by making every possible effort to integrate into the local communities where they lived. (Home Office, 2008, p. 16)

In terms of final assessment, it is worth underlining that in the official political discourse, communitarian and civic republican principles thus characterized New Labour's Third Way politics (Marinetto, 2003), thus challenging the neoliberal notion of active citizenship that was previously promoted by the New Right. In the definition provided by New Labour, active citizenship entailed the establishment of a new relationship with public institutions, not merely based on consumerist principles but founded instead on political and civic patterns. In this sense it was seen as a modality to bring in forms of input legitimacy to government's policy-making, by fostering bottom-up processes based on community engagement and civic participation. This, in our view, is in line with the main trends in Western society and implies the transformation from government to governance, with more powers acquired by subnational institutional and non-institutional policy actors, in order to reduce deficits of democracy that afflict centralized systems (Hooghe & Marks, 2001; Kohler-Koch & Larat, 2009). In the UK this process was put in place in order to shape participatory models of policy-making (Andrews *et al.*, 2008). The key public service reforms driving New Labour's agenda were therefore central in order to improve the overall democratic performance of the political system. However, academic literature argues that this project of reform has not been completely successful (Geddes, 2006; Clarke & Newman, 2007; Davies, 2012) and still maintains neoliberal connotations (Gilbert, 2004; Davies, 2012), with an overall problem being the lack of an adequate transfer of power that can be thought of as creating a 'truly citizen-centred government' (Marinetto, 2003, p. 118). This central point of criticism towards New Labour's approach also emerges from our analysis, as we explain in the final section of this article.

The Interplay Between Public Institutions and Civil Society in Defining Active Citizenship in Britain

In light of the above, the results of a study conducted within the PIDOP project on the position of NGOs and public institutions working in a number of policy areas and targeting a number of relevant social groups (i.e. women, minorities, migrants, and youth) will be presented. The aim of the study was to map their political values and political priorities, and also their positioning with respect to core policies. The analysis furnishes a particularly important evaluation of the establishment of active citizenship under New Labour and sheds light on some critical aspects in regards to improving the social inclusion of traditionally marginalized groups.

Emerging Trends: Values, Political Priorities, and Policy Responses

The priority of New Labour's policies, as outlined in the previous section of this article, was to foster the basis for social inclusion by promoting civic engagement and community cohesion. In our analysis we focused on the actual reach of this policy agenda by investigating first the values and political priorities of the NGO activists and second by focusing on their actual role in the policy process. In this way, our aim was to understand the extent to which the political strategies promoted under New Labour were actually inclusive (of migrants, women, or minorities) or exclusive. In this term, it is particularly relevant to focus on one of the core discursive nodal points that emerge from the overall PIDOP analysis, i.e. the social dimension (see Bee & Guerrina, 2014).

In this regard, a recurring discourse emerging in the NGOs' narrative concerns antidiscrimination policies and equality. This is a theme that, according to interviewees, is not yet prominent in the current political agenda. From the analysis of NGOs' documents the following themes assume key relevance: the importance assigned to the local dimension of the integration policy, the necessity to develop responses aimed at building forms of community cohesion as a strategy to bring together marginalized groups, and the need to build relationships between different networks, strengthen formal and informal social networks, and reduce racial tensions and improve the sense of community identity and common ownership. Active civic engagement is considered to be the instrument to challenge discrimination along with the growth of extreme right extremism, racism, and xenophobia, as we will discuss further below.

Our analysis clearly shows the necessity to bring in measures that create opportunities for involvement and participation at all levels of society for under-represented groups. Addressing the issue of difference and minorities' social inclusion emerge as core priorities for building active citizenship in our data, and they are considered as not taken fully into account when the political agenda is put into practice. In this regard, another prominent priority area is social justice with a particular emphasis given to youth justice. The advocacy aim leading NGOs' activities can be summarized by referring to the position of the national organization 11Million, whose activities are focused on moving 'children and young people into the heart of the decision-making process to increase understanding of their best interests' (11Million, 2009, p. 4) in order to ensure that the 'voices of children and young people are genuinely able to shape and influence national safeguarding policy and practice' (11Million, 2009, p. 10). A particularly significant policy area is education policy and its perspective on citizenship education which includes activities that can foster and improve community cohesion and the fostering of a sense of social solidarity at a local level. The need to take into account the intersection between policies targeting different groups is also addressed, since one of the emerging priorities regards the empowerment of ethnic minority women; in particular, policy actions should be undertaken in order to integrate women from marginalized and disadvantaged backgrounds. In the 2008 submission to the UK National Action Plan, Oxfam UK raised important issues regarding the interconnection between policy areas regarding women, poverty, and social inclusion:

> Tackling women's social exclusion is key to tackling women's poverty. People's experiences of poverty differ according to their gender, as well as their race, age and where they live. And people's needs, assets and the barriers they face in overcoming poverty are also gendered. (Oxfam, 2008, p. 2)

Diversity is posited as something which can also add value to the workplace and the political sphere. The integration of ethnic minority women is necessary and valuable, because it can provide society with skills, competences, and talents, a cultural capital which is unique and otherwise unavailable. When it comes to evaluating the actual implementation of these institutional principles, however, NGO activists are rather sceptical in regards to the actual impact of current policies which, according to their views, follow top-down patterns. This is a particularly important point that looks at the tensions existing between the inclusive and exclusive elements of active citizenship as well as at the rationale underlying the policies of active engagement promoted by New Labour. As we explain in the next section, there is evidence of the fact that the bottom-up processes stimulated by programmes such as the New Deal for Communities are not yet fully inclusive of traditionally marginalized groups, such as ethnic minority women. The empowerment of this social group is thus considered as a key priority in order to challenge discrimination. The set of policy responses and policy recommendations figured out by NGOs in order to promote antidiscrimination and equality rights is closely linked to the second theme outlined in this article, and focuses on the components of active citizenship.

Components of Active Citizenship: The Values of Structured Dialogue and Participatory Democracy

Particularly relevant for the analysis that we carried out in PIDOP is the discussion regarding active citizenship. In line with the PIDOP discursive nodal points (see Bee & Guerrina, 2014), the narratives framing 'participation'—and the modalities to improve it—emerged as a key point of discussion during the interviews with the NGO activists as well as in their policy documents. This is of course coherent, in terms of policy discussion, with the overall strategies promoted under Tony Blair and Gordon Brown. In general, our data show evidence of activists' recognition of the general principles—such as empowerment and active engagement—that represent New Labour's approach to active citizenship. At the same time, however, there is an emerging criticism of its actual setting and effective practice. Overall, it can be argued that this status is still not fully inclusive of the whole society and does not completely consider the participation of marginalized groups. Furthermore, a recurrent narrative emerging from our data is highly critical of recent policy actions, such as the 2008 Green Paper, which are seen as undermining the exercise of active citizenship rather than favouring it.

Activists consider active citizenship as a way to foster democracy and re-engage citizens with decision-making processes; they therefore acknowledge the ideological approach undertaken by New Labour and the civic republican and communitarian elements that characterize the institutional approach to active citizenship. Civil renewal in the UK—as stated, for example, in a report published by NCVO in 2005—focuses on improving the existing interrelationship between voluntary organizations and state institutions by fostering citizens' political participation in public life. In this regard, active citizenship 'implies that citizens have a political relationship with the state, and not simply a consumerist one' (NCVO, 2005, p. 10). This perception is important because it draws a consistent difference with the New Right approach to active citizenship that emerged at the end of the 1980s. New Labour's model of citizenship is discussed and recognized because it is based on the fulfilment of responsibilities, as part of active participation, and an attempt to re-engage citizens. Participatory democracy and deliberative practices at the community level are seen as the instruments to shape the relationship between public institutions and citizens. Commenting upon the Blunkett approach to active citizenship, NCVO argued that:

> New Labour's version of citizenship is more in line with the civic republican model. Citizens are defined by duty: rights of citizens are dependent on the fulfilment of their responsibilities. The emphasis is equally based on active participation. The move from government to governance is about sharing risks and responsibilities between citizens and the state, and expanding democratic participation by re-

engaging citizens with decision making processes. New Labour's take on citizenship is also greatly influenced by the communitarian model: citizen participation in governance is essentially promoted at the community level in wanting to develop participatory democracy. (NCVO, 2005, pp. 8–9)

However, the empowerment of civil society groups dealing with minorities, migrants, women, and youth is seen by activists as necessary in order to set the bases for participatory democracy, but not yet fully integrated in the current policy agenda. In that respect, a number of policy recommendations aiming to improve the approach to active citizenship emerge from our activists' interviews. In particular, intercultural exchange is considered an important means to develop further because of its centrality in social cohesion. One of the drivers of civic engagement mentioned in the documents analysed is in fact the fostering of civil society projects promoting cultural awareness between communities by improving reciprocal understandings between different minorities, addressing racism and inequalities, and raising awareness of discrimination in all areas of society.

Furthermore, participation in community planning and generally in political life at a local level is considered central for the improvement of a communitarian identity and integration of different social groups. Active citizenship is perceived as a driver for fostering community cohesion and for shaping a more integrated society. Our data provide evidence of this, showing that civil society organizations acknowledge—and advocate for—the inclusion of a broader consideration of difference principles in the notion of citizenship. This provides evidence that the principles and values of active citizenship put forward by Blair and Brown are widely recognized by the civil society. There is however a widespread criticism towards the approach undertaken by the New Labour government, as it is considered to be based on 'one-sided engagement'. During an interview, for example, an activist declared that active citizenship:

(...) is very much a one-sided process, where public institutions just ask NGOs to work on issues that interest the national government and there is no partnership in the design or the identification of the important issues. (Interview n. 2, activist of BRAP)

In terms of the policy instruments that should be developed to improve the actual practices of active citizenship and foster a two-sided process especially at a local level, NGOs proposed the increase of consultations with local organizations and the enhancement of civil dialogue. In particular, the following were mentioned: the development of forums, consultations with regional communities, as well as the promotion of civil dialogue between institutional and non-institutional actors representing minorities. Strong emphasis was also placed on the strengthening of local communities through the provision of targeted funding.

Dialogue was also seen as fundamental in building community cohesion, in light of making different communities engage with each other, by favouring the development of positive relationships between minorities and creating opportunities to connect, meet openly, and debate everyday life concerns. Civil dialogue, and this is important to emphasize, was seen as functional to address new emerging social problems, such as political extremism.

For instance, in a *Memorandum of Evidence from the Muslim Council of Britain*, we found evidence of the political discourse regarding the need to enhance democratization processes by engaging in a dialogue with civil society organizations. The overall purpose is to promote active engagement in order to reduce the risk of extremism:

> Prior to 7/7 and even 9/11, British Muslim civil society was evolving to make vibrant contributions to the mainstream third sector. Through active engagement with a range of funding bodies, Muslim community groups could deliver projects on par with other organisations of all faiths and none. (...) There has to be fresh and enlightened thinking on the renewal of democratic processes to make Britain a better nation by strengthening civil society and giving power back to the people, in terms of accountability. (Muslim Council of Britain, 2009, pp. 2, 3)

At the same time, however, the most recent integration policies put forward by Brown's government have been criticized as contradictory and still one-sided. In commenting upon the 2008 Green Paper, the Migrants Rights Network argued that

> The Green Paper strategy is one-sided in considering only the demands to be placed on migrants to assimilate into British society. No consideration is given to the responsibilities and obligations of British society towards migrants. (...) The concept of 'active citizenship' is poorly developed in these proposals. As it exists in the Green Paper it will disadvantage too many candidates for secure residence status. (Migrants Rights Network, 2008, pp. 2, 4)

This strategy is seen as potentially dangerous because it is exclusively biased towards the needs of the host community and because the notion of active citizenship is considered as lacking the communitarian bases that were established in Blunkett's original policy proposal on active citizenship and community cohesion. This is a key issue that still undermines the actual exercise of active citizenship by traditionally marginalized groups.

Conclusion

As it has been argued in this article, the policies of active citizenship promoted in Britain since the late 1980s have been influenced by a series of contextual factors and social problems and determined by different ideological viewpoints that have shifted the meaning and practices of active engagement across time. The version of active citizenship proposed by conservatives in the 1980s had a strong neoliberal connotation: it was highly individualistic and not based on a collectivist understanding of the structure of the welfare (Kearns, 1995, p. 157). It was exclusivist in its own right, and the empowerment of citizens was based on property ownership that favoured the creation of different classes of citizens. In exploration of the actual value of this process, Brehony (1992, p. 204) argued that the 'active citizen was very much a child of its times and, for the most part, it disappeared from the texts of ministers' speeches as the recession began to deepen'.

Political ideas and discourses surrounding active citizenship became prominent again towards the end of the 1990s. Indeed, the civic republican account for citizenship that shaped New Labour policies was initiated by Tony Blair in 1997. From a neoliberal standpoint based on the guarantee of individual freedoms at a community level, active citizenship has assumed communitarian and civic republican characteristics as shaped by the New Labour agenda. Arguments that emerged in the literature however criticized the approach promoted by New Labour across time. Davies (2012), for example, in comparing this approach with the New Right definition of active citizenship, outlines that while there were important differences in modus operandi, each drew on common political principles. In particular, in comparing New Labour's approach to community and deliberation with the Habermasian ideal-typical model of civic engagement and public participation, the scholar outlines a series of critical issues that emerge from a closer analysis of actual policies. Overall, the partnerships developed under New Labour embedded 'the principles of "contributory consensualism"—the duty of citizen activists to mobilize community resources in pursuit of non-negotiable government policies' (Davies, 2012, p. 10). In relation to this, Marinetto argues that New Labour's policies of community involvement 'have not been accompanied by a substantive transfer of executive power from the centre to local institutions and people' (Marinetto, 2003, p. 116). This emerges also from the data that we collected in the PIDOP project that confirm that civil society activists, even if acknowledging the principles of active citizenship put in place by New Labour, are criticizing the top-down logic, based on institutional priorities rather than on social needs that this represents.

In addition, when looking more specifically at the approach to integration policy, it is worth underlining the rather highly exclusionary value that is attributed to active citizenship. Overall the recognition of a set of social problems generated by a failed approach to integration and immigration policy resulted in the promotion of active forms of citizenship by increasing trust and confidence in marginalized communities and in the development of strategies aimed at breaking down barriers and divisions between communities and between minorities and organizations. Although the initial community cohesion strategies and integration policies were criticized due to their assimilationist guiding principles, it is the events of 7/7 and the growth of tensions towards new immigrants in Britain that pushed forward an integration policy based on a path to citizenship entailing the adaptation of minorities into the mainstream cultural setting.

Overall from our research, the criticism of this approach emerges quite prominently both in the analysis of policy documents and in the interviews with NGO activists. The civic republican values of participatory democracy and civic engagement as well as the communitarian principles of cultural and civic identity and solidarity are the principal objectives that influence the activities and values of civil society. Instruments such as civil dialogue are considered key to strategically build community cohesion and shape intercultural exchange between weak and dominant public spheres in Britain. These viewpoints characterize, from our point of view, the basis of a counterdiscourse emerging from civil society activists that criticizes Blunkett's approach to active citizenship as being 'one-sided' and the Brown government's approach as being based exclusively on the commitment of minorities to assimilate with the mainstream culture. Our research places emphasis on the ambiguities inherent in the discussion surrounding the approach to active citizenship over the years. In conclusion, we can argue that the notion that has been put forward does not completely account for the full inclusion of traditionally marginalized groups in civil society and in policy processes.

Funding

Project sponsored by the European Commission's 7th Framework Programme [FP7-SSH-2007-1, grant agreement no. 225282].

References

11Million. (2009) *One-Year Business Plan April 2009—March 2010*. Available at http://dera.ioe.ac.uk/9578/1/force_download.php%3Ffp%3D%252Fclient_assets%252Fcp%252Fpublication%252F374%252F11_MILLION_Business_Plan_2009-10.pdf (accessed 30 March 2013).
Andrews, R., Cowell, R. & Downe, J. (2008) Support for active citizenship and public service performance: An empirical analysis of English local authorities, *Policy & Politics*, 36(2), pp. 225–243.
Atkinson, A. (2003) Addressing urban social exclusion through community involvement in urban regeneration, in: R. Imrie & M. Raco (Eds) *Urban Renaissance? New Labour, Community and Urban Policy*, pp. 101–119 (Bristol: Policy Press).
Bee, C. & Guerrina, R. (2014) Participation, dialogue, and civic engagement: Understanding the role of organized civil society in promoting active citizenship in the European Union, *Journal of Civil Society*, doi:10.1080/17448689.2013.861651.
Bellamy, R. (2000) *Rethinking Liberalism* (London: Pinter).
Bellamy, R., Castiglione, D. & Santoro, E. (2004) *Lineages of European Citizenship. Rights, Belonging and Participation in Eleven Nation-States* (Basingstoke: Palgrave Macmillan).
Brannan, T., John, P. & Stoker, G. (2006) Active citizenship and effective public services and programmes: How can we know what really works?, *Urban Studies*, 43(5–6), pp. 993–1008.
Brehony, K. J. (1992) Active Citizens': The case of school governors, *International Studies in Sociology of Education*, 2(2), pp. 199–217.
Burnett, J. (2007) Britain's 'civilising project': Community cohesion and core values, *Policy and Politics*, 35(2), pp. 353–357.
Carrera, S. & Guild, E. (Eds) (2009) *Illiberal Liberal States: Immigration, Citizenship and Integration in the EU* (Aldershot: Ashgate).
Castles, S. & Davidson, A. (2000) *Citizenship and Migration. Globalisation and the Politics of Belonging* (London: McMillan Press).
Clarke, J. & Newman, J. (2007) What's in a name? New Labour's citizen-consumers and the remaking of public services, *Cultural Studies*, 21(4/5), pp. 738–757.
Davies, J. (2012) Active citizenship: Navigating the conservative heartlands of the New Labour project, *Policy & Politics*, 40(1), pp. 3–19.
Delanty, G. (2000) *Citizenship in a Global Age* (Buckingham: Open University Press).
Delanty, G. (2007) European citizenship: A critical assessment, *Citizenship Studies*, 11(1), pp. 63–72.
Dinam, A. (2005) Empowered or over powered? Real experiences of local participation in the UK's new deal for communities, *Community Development Journal*, 40(3), pp. 301–312.
Drake, R. F. (2001) *The Principles of Social Policy* (London: Palgrave Macmillan).
Eder, K. & Giesen, G. (Eds) (2001) *European Citizenship Between National Legacies and Postnational Projects* (Oxford: Oxford University Press).
Etzioni, A. (1993) *The Spirit of Community* (New York: Crown Publishers).
Etzioni, A. (1995) *New Communitarian Thinking* (Charlottesville: University of Virginia Press).
Faulks, K. (1998) *Citizenship in Modern Britain* (Edinburg: Edinburgh University Press).
Faulks, K. (2000) *Citizenship* (London: Routledge).
Fraser, N. (1992) Rethinking the public sphere: A contribution to the critique of actually existing democracy, in: C. Calhoun (Ed.) *Habermas and the Public Sphere*, pp. 109–142 (Cambridge, MA: MIT Press).
Fyfe, N. R. (1993) Making space for the citizen? The (in)significance of the UK citizen's charter, *Urban Geography*, 14(3), pp. 224–227.
Fyfe, N. R. (1995) Law and order policy and the spaces of citizenship in contemporary Britain, *Political Geography*, 14(2), pp. 177–189.
Geddes, M. (2006) Partnership and the limits to local governance in England: Institutionalist analysis and neoliberalism, *International Journal of Urban and Regional Research*, 30(1), pp. 76–97.
Giddens, A. (1998) *The Third Way. The Renewal of Social Democracy* (Cambridge: Polity Press).

Giddens, A. (2000) *The Third Way and Its Critics* (Cambridge: Polity Press).
Giddens, A. (Ed.) (2001) *The Global Third Way Debate* (Cambridge: Polity Press).
Giddens, A. (2006) Positive welfare, in: C. Pierson & F. G. Castles (Eds) *The Welfare State Reader*, pp. 378–388 (Cambridge: Polity Press).
Gilbert, J. (2004) The second wave: The specificity of New Labour neoliberalism, *Soundings*, (26), pp. 25–45.
Habermas, J. (1994) Citizenship and national identity, in: B. Van Steenbergen (Ed.) *The Condition of Citizenship*, pp. 20–35 (London: Sage).
Habermas, J. (1996) *Between Facts and Norms: Contributions to a Discourse Theory of Law and Democracy* (Oxford: Polity Press).
Heater, D (1991) Citizenship: A remarkable case of sudden interest, *Parliamentary Affairs*, 44(2), pp. 140–156.
Heater, D. (1999) *What Is Citizenship?* (Cambridge: Polity Press).
Home Office. (2001) *Community Cohesion: A Report of the Independent Review Team Chaired by Ted Cantle*. Available at http://resources.cohesioninstitute.org.uk/Publications/Documents/Document/DownloadDocumentsFile.aspx?recordId=96&file=PDFversion (accessed 30 March 2013).
Home Office. (2002) *Secure Borders, Safe Haven. Integration with Diversity in Modern Britain*. Available at http://www.archive2.official-ocuments.co.uk/document/cm53/5387/cm5387.pdf (accessed 30 March 2013).
Home Office. (2008) *The Path to Citizenship: Next Steps in Reforming the Immigration System*. Available at http://webarchive.nationalarchives.gov.uk/20100422120657/http:/www.ukba.homeoffice.gov.uk/sitecontent/documents/aboutus/consultations/pathtocitizenship/pathtocitizenship?view=Binary#page=1&zoom=auto,0,849 (accessed 30 March 2013).
Hooghe, L. & Marks, G. (2001) *Multilevel Governance and European Integration* (Boulder, Colorado: Rowman & Littlefield).
Hurd, D. (1989) Active citizenship, in: Digitised Editions of Commons and Lords Hansard. Available at http://hansard.millbanksystems.com/written_answers/1989/feb/02/active-citizenship#S6CV0146P0_19890202_CWA_237 (accessed 1 September 2013).
Isin, E. F., Nyers, P. & Turner, B. S. (2009) *Citizenship Between Past and Future* (London: Routledge).
Kearns, A. (1995) Active citizenship and local governance: Political and geographical dimensions, *Political Geography*, 14(2), pp. 155–175.
Keith, M. (1989) Riots as a social problem in British cities, in: D. T. Herbert & D. M. Smith (Eds) *Social Problems and the City: New Perspectives*, pp. 289–306 (Oxford: Oxford University Press).
Kohler-Koch, B. & Larat, B. (Eds) (2009) *European Multi-Level Governance. Contrasting Images in National Research* (Cheltenham: Edward Elgar).
Kymlicka, W. (1995) *Multicultural Citizenship* (Oxford: Clarendon Press).
Lister, R. (1997) *Citizenship: Feminist Perspectives* (Basingstoke: MacMillan).
Lister, R. (2007) Citizenship, in: G. Blakeley & V. Bryson (Eds) *The Impact of Feminism on Political Concepts and Debates*, pp. 57–72 (Manchester: Manchester University Press).
MacKian, S. (1995) That great dust-heap called history: Recovering the multiple spaces of citizenship, *Political Geography*, 14(2), pp. 209–216.
Marinetto, M. (2003) Who wants to be an active citizen? The politics and practice of community involvement, *Sociology*, 37(1), pp. 103–120.
Marshall, T. H. (1950) *Citizenship and Social Class: And Other Essays* (Cambridge: University Press).
Marston, S. A. (1995) The private goes public: Citizenship and the new spaces of civil society, *Political Geography*, 14(2), pp. 194–198.
McGhee, D. (2003) Moving to 'our' common ground—A critical examination of community cohesion discourse in twenty-first century Britain, *The Sociological Review*, 51(3), pp. 376–404.
McGhee, D. (2006) Getting 'host' communities on board: Finding the balance between 'managed migration' and 'managed settlement' in community cohesion strategies, *Journal of Ethnic and Migration Studies*, 32(1), pp. 111–127.
McGhee, D. (2008) *The End of Multiculturalism? Terrorism, Integration and Human Rights* (Berkshire: Open University Press).
McGhee, D. (2009) The paths to citizenship: A critical examination of immigration policy in Britain since 2001, *Patterns of Prejudice*, 43(1), pp. 41–64.
Migrants Rights Network. (2008) *The Path to Citizenship. Commenting on the Home Office Green Paper*. Available at http://www.migrantsrights.org.uk/files/publications/path_to_citizenship.pdf (accessed 30 March 2013).
Miller, D. (2000) *Citizenship and National Identity* (Cambridge: Polity Press).

Miller, D. (2008a) Immigrants, nations and citizenship, *Journal of Political Philosophy*, 16(4), pp. 371–390.
Miller, D. (2008b) Republican citizenship, nationality and Europe, in: C. Laborde & J. Maynor (Eds) *Republicanism and Political Theory*, pp. 133–158 (Oxford: Wiley-Blackwell).
Modood, T. (2007) *Multiculturalism: A Civic Idea* (Cambridge: Polity Press).
Mouffe, C. (1992) Democratic citizenship and the political community, in: C. Mouffe (Ed.) *Dimensions of Radical Democracy: Pluralism, Citizenship, Community*, pp. 225–239 (London: Verso).
Mulvey, G. (2010) When policy creates politics: The problematizing of immigration and the consequences for refugee integration in the UK, *Journal of Refugee Studies*, 23(4), pp. 437–462.
Muslim Council of Britain. (2009) *Memorandum of Evidence from the Muslim Council of Britain. Communities and Local Government Committee: Preventing Violent Extremism*. Available at http://www.mcb.org.uk/downloads/MCB_Submission_Prevent.pdf (accessed 30 March 2013).
NCVO. (2005) *Civil Renewal and Active Citizenship: A Guide to the Debate*. Available at http://www.ncvo-vol.org.uk/sites/default/files/UploadedFiles/NCVO/Publications/Publications_Catalogue/Sector_Research/civil_renewal_active_citizenship.pdf (accessed 30 March 2013).
Oliver, D. (1991) Active citizenship in the 1990s, *Parliamentary Affairs*, 44(2), pp. 157–171.
Oxfam. (2008) *Women and Social Exclusion: Oxfam Submission to NAP 2008*. Available at http://policy-practice.oxfam.org.uk/publications/women-and-social-exclusion-oxfam-submission-to-nap-2008-112332 (accessed 30 March 2013).
Pateman, C. (1988) *The Sexual Contract* (Cambridge: Polity Press).
Phillimore, J. (2012) Implementing integration in the UK: Lessons for integration theory, policy and practice, *Policy & Politics*, 40(4), pp. 525–545.
Ratcliffe, P. (2012) Community cohesion: Reflections on a flawed paradigm, *Critical Social Policy*, 32(2), pp. 262–281.
Robinson, D. (2005) The search for community cohesion: Key themes and dominant concepts of the public policy agenda, *Urban Studies*, 42(8), pp. 1411–1427.
Roche, M. (1992) *Rethinking Citizenship: Welfare, Ideology and Change in Modern Society* (Cambridge: Polity Press).
Smith, S. J. (1995) Citizenship: All or nothing, *Political Geography*, 14(2), pp. 190–193.
Stevenson, N. (2001) *Culture and Citizenship* (London: Sage).
Taylor, C. (1989) *Sources of the Self: The Making of the Modern Identity* (Cambridge: Cambridge University Press).
Walzer, M (1983) *Spheres of Justice* (Oxford: Blackwell).
Worley, C. (2005) It's not about race. It's about the community: New Labour and 'community cohesion', *Critical Social Policy*, 4(25), pp. 483–496.
Wright, J. S. F., Parry, J., Mathers, J., Jones, S. & Orford, J. (2006) Assessing the participatory potential of Britain's new deal for communities, *Policy Studies*, 27(4), pp. 347–361.
Young, I. M. (1990) *Justice and the Politics of Difference* (Princeton: Princeton University Press).

Index

Note: Page numbers in **bold** type refer to figures
Page numbers in *italic* type refer to tables
Page numbers followed by 'n' refer to notes

Action for Justice and Peace (2008) 57
active citizenship 106–9; definitions 101; European Commission-sponsored policy 32; European Union 29–50; Great Britain 109–13; local policy actors 30; New Labour 107, 112; New Right Political Discourse 104–6; public domain 2; values 2; values of structured dialogue 111–13
actors: European Public Sphere (EPS) 34–7; local policy 30
Amnå, E.: and Ekman, J. 70
anti-discrimination: ENAR 45
asymmetrical influence 35
Ataman, A.: *et al.* 76
Ayata, A.: and Tütüncü, F. 72

Barbosa, C.: and Zobel, C. 53
Barrett, M.: and Brunton-Smith, I. 2, 5–28; and Pachi, D. 70; and Zani, B. 70
Beacon of Democracy 51–9
Bee, C.: and Guerrina, R. 2–4, 29–50; and Pachi, D. 3, 100–16; and Scartezzino, R. 86
Bertocchi, A.: and Villano, P. 3, 82–99
biodirectional influences 14
biodirectional institutional communication model 36, **36**
Blunkett, D. 108
bottom-up processes: young people 91
Brehoney, K. 104, 105, 113
British Muslim civil society 113
Brunton-Smith, I.: and Barrett, M. 2, 5–28
Brussels-based organizations 44–5

Calhoun, C. 33
Carvalhais, I. 52; integration concept 66n
Castells, M. 31, 34

children and young people: national safeguarding policy 110
citizen-centred strategy: public policy approach 47
citizens: Eastern Europe 9
Citizens Charter 105
citizenship: communitarian 102; concept 83; definitions 101; framing definitions 101–2; good 15; Italy 84; nationality 86; neoliberal perspective 102; New Labour 111; policies; relating to youth and migrants (Portugal) 51–69; processes and values 90; programme 2; social idea 101; women's rights 75
civic activity 22
civic engagement: mechanisms 100–14; participatory democracy 106
civic identity 103
civic participation: definition 6; diverse types of activities 6, *7*
civil dialogue 48n; political participation 42–4; Social Platform 42
civil movement: Turkey 80n
civil society 32–4, 64; British Muslim 113; empowerment 2, 112; Europeanization 34–5; organizations 41; organized 29–50; public institutions 109–13
civil society actors: institutions 2
Civil Society Development Centre 71
civil society discourses: national policies 54
civil society statements: policy documents 43
class analysis 22
classroom climate: education 11
cognitive factors 15
collective action: identity threat 20
collective efficacy 15–16
Colombo, A. 94

INDEX

communication: bidirectional institutional model 36, **36**; debates 40
communitarian citizenship 102
community: cohesion 106, 112; engagement and empowerment 107; hard to reach 52; planning 112; role of individual 104
Constitutional Treaty (EU, 2005) 39, 47; failure 63
Cooperation for Development of the Emerging Countries (COSPE) 95, 96
counter-discourse: EuroActive 39, 40
countries: characteristics 9; demographic consistencies 19; participation 21
criminalisation: illegal immigration 85
critical discourse analysis 31

Davies, J. 114
debates: communication 40
decentralized states: engagement and participation 9
decision-making mechanisms: socio-economic conditions 42
deliberative democracy 103
democratization: public sphere 39–41
demographic consistencies: countries 19
demographic factors 13–18; complex patterns 22; engagement and participation 9; ethnicity 9; socioeconomic status (SES) 9; voting 22–3
depoliticization: Turkey 70
devolution 101
Diez, J. 32, 34, 44
Disciplinary Code of the Higher Education Credit and Dormitories Institution (Yurt-Kur) 78
discourse analysis 31–2
discourses: policy development 38–9, *38*; policy makers 62; review 70; young people 63; youth and migrants (Italy) 82–99
discrimination: perceived 20
discursive battleground: Europe as (Diez) 44
discursive nodal points (DNPs) 31, 32, **32**, 40; European institutional discourse 38; four types 41
discursive structure 54

Eastern Europe: citizens 9
education: classroom climate 11; engagement and participation 10, 11; political knowledge 11
education programmes: information campaigns 46
efficacy: high external 20
Ekman, J.: and Amnå, E. 70
electoral system: engagement and participation 8; voter turnout 8
elite interviews: women and youth 77

emblematic issues: theoretical-methodological approach 54
emotional factors 16
employment: formal (Italy) 93; and poverty 78
empowerment: civil society 2, 112; and community engagement 107; information 42; women 75, 79
ENAR (European Network Against Racism) 40–1, 43, 44, 45, 46
engagement and participation: decentralized states 9; demographic factors 9; education 10, 11; electoral system 8; ethnicity 9; family 10; gender 10; labour force 10; macro-contextual factors 8; mass media 12; minority and migrant groups 9; non-political organizations 12; patterns of 8–13; peer groups 12–13; population features 8; social factors 10; voter turnout 8; women 9; workplace 12
equality: gender 45, 48n, 75; principles 87
ethnicity: demographic factors 9; engagement and participation 9
Euro-sceptic movement 63
EuroActive: counter-discourse 39, 40
Eurobarometer data: analysis 19
Europe: hard to reach communities 52; identity 32–4, 57; institutions 35; integration 54, 61, 91; Italian policies 97; member states 1; public institutions 41; social dimension 44–6
European Commission 39–40, 92; citizenship definition 83; Constitutional Treaty (2005) 30, 39; initiatives 61; (2004–10) 38
European Commission-sponsored policy: active citizenship 32
European discourses: PIs and NGOs documents 57
European Discursive Battleground 34, 47
European governance: Lisbon Treaty (Article 11) 43; umbrella organizations 37
European institutional discourse: discursive nodal points (DNP) 38
European Parliament (EP) 66n
European Public Sphere (EPS) 30, 32, 33, 39, 46; actors 34–7
European Social Dimension 44–6
European Social Forum (ESF) 35
European Union (EU): active citizenship 29–50, 37–46; application of principles 52; Lisbon Treaty (Article 11) 2, 30, 43, 64; policy 65; projects development 63; Youth Policy (EYF) 42, 44; Youth Strategy 55
European-level organized civil society 41
Europeanization 33, 34; civic society 34–5; globalization 101; transnationalization 41–2
EWL (European Women's Lobby) 45, 46
external efficacy 15

INDEX

EYF (EU Youth Policy) 42; mechanisms of engagement 42; Young People and Poverty 44

family: discourses and social factors 14; engagement and participation 10; social factors 10
family-centred governmental approach 72
Faulks, K. 105
feminist movements: Turkey 72
Fernandes-Jesus, M.: et al. 51–68
foreign-born immigrants 53
formal employment: Italy 93
Fraser, N. 1, 103

Galligan, Y. 10
gender: difference and participation 22; engagement and participation 10; voter turnout 10
gender equality 45, 48n; policies 45; Turkey 75
Gender Equality Action Plan (Turkey) 74
generational status: minority and migrant groups 10
global citizenship: young people 56
globalization 101
good citizenship: beliefs 15
governance: European 37, 43; literature 31; local 104; White Paper (EC, 2001) 47
government: efficiency 22; family-centred approach 72
Grassi, M. 53
Great Britain (GB) 102; active citizenship 109–13; Home Office 108–9
Grimm, D. 33
Guerrina, R.: and Bee, C. 2–4, 29–50

Habermas, J. 33, 103
Habermasian model 33
Hajer, M. 31; and Wagenaar, H. 31
hard to reach communities: Europe 52
Hess, R.D.: and Torney, J.V. 12
Home Office (UK) 108–9
house girl 80n
Humana Global document (2006) 56, 57
Hurd, D. 104

identity: civic 103; European 32–4, 57
identity threat: collective action 20
illegal immigration: criminalization 85
Immigrant Solidarity Association 59; interviews 60
immigrants: foreign-born 53
immigration policy 53; racist 59
indirect mobilizing channels 12–13
individual: role in community 104

influence: balance of 14; policy process 33; potential sources 14
information: campaigns 46; empowerment 42
institutional communications 36
institutional political strategies 100–14
institutional trust 15, 20
institutions: civil society sectors 2, *see also* PIs (public institutions)
integrated causal psychological model of participation 17, **17**
integration: European 54, 61, 91; migrants 97; policies on defence and migrants 58; policy 106; young migrants 85
integration concept (Carvalhais) 66n
Integration of Immigrants Plan (EU) 58
integrative model: political and civic participation and engagement **13**, 14
interactions 36
internal efficacy 15, 22
International Solidarity Association: interviews 60; Youth in Action 60
international surveys: Processes Influencing Democratic Ownership and Participation (PIDOP) 18
intersectionality: organizations 45
interviews: document analysis 65; Immigrant Solidarity Association 60; International Solidarity Association 60; NGO leaders 60–2; SOS Racism 60
Italian Constitution: national legislative framework 87
Italian policies: Europe 97; youth and migration 84, 89–90
Italy: citizenship 84; Democratic Party 90–1; demographic 84; Emilia Romagna Regional Law (no 14) 88; formal employment 93; migrants 93–6; migration 94; Ministry for Youth Policies and Sports Activities (POGAS) 88; National Civil Service Law (no 64) 89; naturalization 85; non-governmental organizations (NGOs) 92, 95; social inclusion 94; voting rights 85, 93; young migrants 94; youth and migrants 82–99
ius sanguinis 65, 84

Koopmans, R. 53
KSGM 74
Kurtaran, Y.: et al. 76
Kymlicka, W. 102

labour force: engagement and participation 10
Laclau, E.: and Mouffe, C. 1
Lisbon Treaty (Article 11) 2, 30, 43, 64
Lister, R. 102
local governance 104

INDEX

local policy actors: active citizenship 30
London Bombing (7/7) 108, 113

McGhee, D. 108
macro contextual factors 9, 13–18; engagement and participation 8; multi-level modelling 20; two main types 13
MAGEEQ project: policy tracing 31
Major, J.: governments 106
Malafaia, C.: *et al.* 51–68
Marinetto, M. 103
Marshall, T. 102, 104
mass media: engagement and participation 12
media 41; discourse 84; news stories 41
Memorandum of Evidence from Muslim Council of Britain (2009) 113
Menezes, I.: *et al.* 51–68
methodological considerations 31–2
migrant integration: Italy 93
Migrant Integration Policy Index III 64
migrants 58–62; African 59; defence of integration policies 58; and ethnic minorities 53; immigration policy 59; integration 97; Italy 93–6; social inclusion 96; values 58; young 85, 94
migrants and youth: Italy 82–99; Portugal 51–69
migration: Italy 94
minority and migrant groups: engagement and participation 9; generational status 10; patterns of participation 9
minority rights: cultural 102
minority youths 9–10
mobilisation: prosocial civic participation 12
modernity development: objectives 74
moral values: psychological literature 97
Mouffe, C.: and Laclau, E. 1
multi-level modelling 21–2, *21*; macro contextual factors 20
Muslim Council of Britain: *Memorandum of Evidence* (2009) 113

National Federation of Youth Associations (FNAJ) 56, 57
national policies: civil society discourses 54
national safeguarding policy: children and young people 110
National Youth Forum 89
nationality 86
naturalization: Italy 85
NCVO 111
neo-republican citizenship 103
neoliberal perspective 103; citizenship 102
network society 31
networked public sphere 34
Neves, T.: *et al.* 51–68

New Labour 106–9; active citizenship 107, 112, 114; citizenship 111; definition of active citizenship 114; policy responses 109–11; political priorities 109–11; Third Way politics 109; values 109–11
New Right government 101
New Right Political Discourse: active citizenship 104–6
news stories 41
Nie, N.H.: *et al.* 11
Nobel Peace Prize (2012) 51–2
non-conventional participation 20
non-governmental organizations (NGOs) 1, 43, 56, 101; activities 1; Italy 92, 95; leaders 60–2, 64; PIDOP project 109, 112; PIs 59; representative 91–2; women 74
non-political organizations: engagement and participation 12
Nussbaum, M. 97

Oliver, D. 105
open consultation: public policy 40
opinionation 20
organizations: Brussels-based 44–5; civil society 41; intersectionality 45
organized civil society (OCS) 30, 34–7, 38, 42, 43, 46; European level 41

Pachi, D.: and Barrett, M. 70; and Bee, C. 3, 100–16
paradoxical movement 52
participation: countries 21; descriptive analyses 19; four distinct types 18, 19; gender difference 22; integrated causal psychological model 17, **17**; non-conventional 20; patterns 9, 10, 22
participatory democracy 106
participatory revolution 52
Path to Citizenship Green Paper (2008) 108
peer groups: engagement and participation 12–13
perceived discrimination 20
PIDOP (Processes Influencing Democratic Ownership and Participation) 3, 5–6, 18–23, 29, 65, 70, 79, 80n, 90, 107, 111, 114; international surveys 18; key parts 71; key policy development 37; NGOs 109, 112; Seventh Framework Programme 6; White Paper on Communications Policy 38
PIs (public institutions) 54–5, 57, 58, 59; civil society 109–13
policy development: discourses 38–9, *38*
policy documents: civil society statements 43
policy makers 62–4; discourses 62; National Action Plan for Social Inclusion (PNAI) 62; NGO leaders 62

INDEX

policy process 33
political capital 15
political and civic participation and engagement: integrative model **13**
political courage 61
political knowledge 11
political participation: civil dialogue 42–4; definition 6; different forms 6, 7; five important dimensions 83; multi-level factor 23
political rights: access to 52
poor neighbourhoods: Turkey 75
population features: engagement and participation 8
Portugal 3, 63; citizenship policies (youth and migrants) 51–69; High Commissioner for Immigration and Intercultural Dialogue (ACIDI) 58; National Action Plan for Social Inclusion (PNAI) 62; Network of Youth for Equal Opportunities between Women and Men (2006) 56; parliament 62; Roadmap for Youth 55, 57; UNDP (2009) 64
post-national citizenship 52
post-structuralism 31
poverty and employment: young people 78
power concentration: umbrella organizations 37
power relations 31
Prodi, R. 97
prosocial civic participation 12; mobilization 12
psychological concept: sense of community 16
psychological factors 15, 19, 23; compromising engagement 16–17; structural equation modelling 19
psychological interventions 23
psychological literature: moral values 97
public communication management 32–4
public domain: active citizenship 2
public policy 103; citizen-centred strategy 47; open consultation 40
public relations: symmetrical model 35
public sphere: concept 40; construction 32–4; democratization 39–41; networked 34

racist immigration policies 59
Ratcliffe, P. 108
realpolitik 61, 64
reciprocity principle 53
research literature: review 6–18
Rete G2-Second Generations 85, 86
Return Directive 52, 64
Ribeiro, N.: *et al.* 3, 51–68
rights: minority 102; political 52; voting 85, 93; women's 75

safeguarding: children and young people 110
Scartezzino, R.: and Bee, C. 86
Schlesinger, P. 34
Sciolla, L. 84
Secure Borders, Safe Haven White Paper (UK, 2002) 108
Sener, T. 69–81
sense of community: psychological concept 16
Smith, J. 108
social cohesion: Independent Review Team Report (Home Office, 2001) 107
social constructivists 31
social exclusion: women 110
social factors 13–18; engagement and participation 10; family discourses 14
social forces 90
social idea: citizenship 101
social identification 16
social inclusion 110; Italy 94; migrants 96; three key issues 95
Social Platform: civil dialogue 42
social policy 44; priorities 95
societal engagement: youth 55
socioeconomic conditions: decision-making mechanisms 42
socioeconomic status (SES): demographic factors 9
SOS Racism 60, 61
structural equation modelling 19; psychological factors 19
symmetrical model: public relations 35

Taylor, C.: and Walzer, M. 102
Teorell, J.: *et al.* 83
Thatcher, M.: government 106
Theiss-Morse, E.: *et al.* 15
theoretical-methodological approach: emblematic issues 54
Third Way 106, 109
Torney, J.V.: and Hess, R.D. 12
Torney–Purta, J.: *et al.* 15
transnationalization 41–2
Tsutsui, K.: and Wotipka, C. 75
Turkey: Civil Law 76; civil movement 80n; Constitution (Article 58) 73; Constitution Coup (1970) 70; depoliticization 70; feminist movements 72; gender equality 75; Gender Equality Action Plan 74; General Directorate on Status of Women 72; Ministry of Family and Social Policies (MoFSP) 72; Ministry of Youth and Sports 72; National Agency 73; policy environment 71; poor neighbourhoods 75; Regulations on Youth Centres 76; Revised European Charter for Youth Participation in Local and Regional Life 77; women and youth 69–81; youth 76–7; youth participation and engagement 72
Tütüncü, F.: and Ayata, A. 72

INDEX

umbrella organizations 37
United Kingdom (UK): National Action Plan (2008) 110
United Nations Development Programme (UNDP, 2009) 64

values: active citizenship 2; migrants 58; New Labour 109–11; of structured dialogue 111–13; youth policy 55
Villano, P.: and Bertocchi, A. 3, 82–99
voter intention 19
voter turnout 8; gender 10
voting 21, 22; demographic factors 22–3; rights (Italy) 85, 93

Wagenaar, H.: and Hajer, M. 31
Walzer, M.: and Taylor, C. 102
Western Europe 103
women: citizenship rights 75; dominant public perspective 75; empowerment 75, 79; engagement and participation 9; EWL (European Women's Lobby) 45, 46; non-governmental organizations (NGOs) 74; social exclusion 110
women and youth: elite interviews 77; Turkey 69–81

workplace: engagement and participation 12
Wotipka, C.: and Tsutsui, K. 75

Young, I. 102
young migrants: integration issues 85; Italy 94
young people 90–3; bottom-up processes 91; discourses 63; global citizenship 56; national safeguarding policy 110; poverty and employment 78; Youth in Action 42
Young People and Poverty (EYF) 44
youth: guarantee of future 77; issues in societal engagement 55; Italian policy 84; Italy 84; minority 9–10; participation and engagement in Turkey 72; period of life 77; Turkey 76–7
Youth in Action 42, 57, 60
youth and migrants: Italy 82–99; Portugal 51–69
Youth Ministry (Italy): organizational history 88

Zani, B.: and Barrett, M. 70
Zobel, C.: and Barbosa, C. 53
Zomeren, M. van: *et al.* 16
Zukin, C.: *et al.* 6, 11, 15